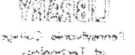

# CAN DEMOCRACY BE TAUGHT?

*Edited by*
*Andrew Oldenquist*

Published by
Phi Delta Kappa Educational Foundation
Bloomington, Indiana, U.S.A.

Cover design by Victoria Voelker

Library of Congress Catalog Card Number 96-68281
ISBN 0-87367-489-8

# TABLE OF CONTENTS

## Part III: Other Societies, Other Problems

# INTRODUCTION

The central question embodied in the title of this collection, "Can democracy be taught?" must move us, first, to examine what we mean by the term *democracy*. If democracy as a concept is not discussed openly, then individuals with different philosophies of democracy will likely find that they are unable to agree about the nature of education *for* democracy. The question of the nature of democracy is especially important for countries that have not experienced democracy, for countries in which political leaders push at the edges of the concept to be able to call a home-grown governance system "democratic," and in countries where the term *democracy* has become a meaningless catchword.

The essays in this volume were written by authors from the United States, South Africa, Germany, and Russia. They were developed as papers that were presented at a 1993 conference on Education for Democracy at Ohio State University, sponsored by the university's Mershon Center, and have been rewritten and expanded for this volume. The authors' areas of expertise include civic education, the problems of minorities, the American Constitution, the transition to democracy in former communist countries, and education and democracy in South Africa and in Japan.

All of the authors concern themselves with aspects of the *ideal of democracy*: what it is, how it evolves, and the goals of democracy yet to be achieved in various settings. Each author implies that democracy has a concrete definition with a range of features. Thus each author also posits that certain social arrangements are democratic while others are not, regardless of the imprimatur of "democracy" applied by a government. Just as the National Socialism of Nazi Germany was no form of socialism, so the People's Democratic Republic of Afghanistan is no form of democracy, in spite of its name.

Readers should note another distinction: Education *for* democracy is not the same as democratic education. In the United States some educators argue that if schools are not democratic, then students will not learn democracy. Others argue that schools cannot be "little democracies" if students are to acquire the character and knowledge, including knowledge of democracy, that they need to be successful. The same problem, from a different angle, is whether democratic education can be consistent with moral education, because the latter, some critics argue, requires directive training (also called "inculcating," "indoctrinating," "fostering," and so on). "Truly democratic" education, and hence education for democracy, would allow children to make their own choices about the "values" they will adopt, wouldn't it? Is not indoctrination just the authoritarian practice in which non-democratic governments or institutions engage when they allow only "politically correct" newspapers and books to be published? Is it more or less serious to limit options for children than it is to restrict the reading of adults? These questions may sound facetious, but they point to the serious question of whether education should be a democratic process.

In *Part I: The New Demography*, Nathan Glazer, Maxine Greene, Joel Kupperman, and Bernard Watson tackle aspects of education for democracy. Nathan Glazer questions the relevance of truth, rather than its objectivity. He asks if truth is the only test of what belongs in a curriculum. Quite apart from Glazer's exploration of the idea that some truths might be harmful and some falsehoods — "myths, fantasies" — might be helpful, his answer is clearly "no." But we must select *which* truths to teach, and our politics, ideals, and moral goals determine this. The trouble with well-intentioned myths — Plato calls them "noble lies" — is that when they are revealed as lies, then the ends they served are discredited.

Glazer also talks about the nature of loyalty, pointing out, for example, that special loyalties in a parochial or Afrocentric school may still be consistent with national loyalty. He asks the excellent question, What do we mean by "self" in "self-esteem"? A person is many selves, contends Glazer. Is only the racial or ethnic self to be represented in the curriculum?

Maxine Greene's ideal of democracy is the creation of "public space," that is, philosophical "space," wherein diverse individuals recognize each other as equals and communicate with each other. In constructing this space, she offers an account, drawn mostly from literature and rich with examples and detail, of the kinds of lives and experiences that are not, or only recently have become, part of the mainstream school curriculum. Today one cannot go through college without being asked to read numerous writers representing women and minority groups who were not repre-sented in the literary canon of 30 years ago. Is there is a danger in replacing stories that have presumably universal messages with so-called victims' stories and in substituting a search for impeccable representation for the search for what is best in liter-ature? Greene believes, "We cannot settle for conditioning" in building a democratic community.

In his essay on pluralism, Joel Kupperman seeks to preserve what is good and right in multiculturalism and to expose what is silly or harmful. He rejects relativism by saying that the world's best music was written by dead, male Germans and Austrians, and at the same time makes a case for increasing the effects of multicultural education. Kupperman offers "perspectivism," say-ing that while it is not quite relativism, it is a useful treatment for self-righteousness and smugness.

Bernard Watson tackles the task of educating disadvantaged children. He believes that equality of opportunity is at the core of what America stands for. He asks, Why, then, does inequality persist? Watson makes the case that millions of poor children lack this kind of equality and argues that it is necessary in a mature democracy that all children share equally in life's starting points.

3

*Part II: Constitutional Imperatives*, includes essays by John Patrick and Kermit Hall. John Patrick believes that learning about the American Constitution and the debates of America's founders are an essential part of any civic education program. The inclusion of these elements forces students to think about the ends of government and the great task, in a democracy, of balancing the government's power and individual freedom in a system of "ordered liberty." Patrick strives to persuade us to his conviction that the best understanding of our complex system comes from studying how the founding era illuminates the problems of the present and, in particular, the "three paradoxes" of how to achieve liberty and order, how to have majority rule and minority rights, and how to secure the public good and the rights of private individuals.

Kermit Hall argues for comparing the American Constitution with foreign constitutions, and then comparing our federal and state constitutions with each other. The U.S. Constitution, Hall says, places greater emphasis on individual rights than on group rights, which is why the United States needs more lawyers than other countries need. Most Third World countries have "social constitutions" that explicitly mention social and ethnic rights, whereas ours does not. Similarly, the American Bill of Rights contains little detail but is judicially interpreted and enforced, while Third World counterparts often contain much detail but are little enforced. For example, Hall says, the United States alone does not prohibit hate speech. A contrasting example that readily comes to mind is the German postwar "Auschwitz Lie Law," which made it a crime to say or write that Auschwitz was *not* an extermination camp.

In *Part III: Other Societies, Other Problems,* the writers address the problems and possibilities in emerging democracies. Essayists in this section include Wolfgang Mitter, Abdusalam Gusseinov, Harold Herman, and William Cummings. Wolfgang Mitter's essay reveals the difficulty of efforts to create (or restore) democracy in Central and Eastern Europe. Mitter quotes Vaclav Havel, president of the Czech Republic, who says that the communist governments of Eastern Europe dissolved morality, replacing morals with external social control; and when political and social freedom came and the external controls were loosened, immorality and crime went wild. The disorder in Central and Eastern Europe, Havel believes, is a result of removing harsh social discipline without adequate preparation for self-discipline and responsibility, which take years to develop. Mitter's central question is, How can the people of Eastern Europe overcome their socialist past? He offers a vivid picture of the immense burden and difficulty of renovating education in the face of poor material resources and a burdensome political legacy.

Abdusalam Gusseinov's five-part characterization of Soviet education portrays its statist, anti-individualist, and totalitarian goals. Gusseinov argues that the ends of that system of education were much less to benefit its recipients than to produce skilled servants of the state and a minimum of dissent. In point four of this characterization, he states the Platonic-paternalistic position: It is right that we are forced to do certain things because they are for our own good, even when it seems to us that they are not. Gusseinov offers limited approval of the communist educational system on a point that should receive the attention of American educators: The very high standards that were set resulted in higher performance, and Gusseinov concludes laconically that, "It is probably natural that results are as high as the goals are harder."

Harold Herman's analysis of the history of apartheid in South Africa before and during the transition to democracy raises important issues and disturbing questions about what people in the Third World mean by "democracy." Herman says, with considerable backing, that developing and previously oppressed populations value equality and community higher than freedom and individualism. The former values, he says, are part of a preliberal notion of democracy that has it roots in the philosophy of Rousseau. Herman's account of the "liberation now, education later" movement is fascinating reading.

William Cummings concludes this section. In his essay he posits that Japanese education promotes democracy and egalitarianism but not individualism, and that its egalitarianism has been limited. Cummings comments, for example, "Postwar Japanese education has promoted class equality but not gender equality." Thus, as he examines the democratic ideals of Japan and several other Asian countries, Cummings harkens to the notion of the democratic "perspectives" that also are explored by Greene and Kupperman.

# PART I

# The New Demography

# Five Questions About Multiculturalism

## BY NATHAN GLAZER

The conflict over multiculturalism has been waged vigorously in many arenas in the United States. In this essay I deal with the intense debate that has been going on now for a half-dozen years or more, and still goes on, over the content of the social studies in elementary and secondary schools and how that content should reflect or take account of American ethnic and racial diversity.

Nowhere perhaps has the dispute been sharper than in New York State, where a few years ago Thomas Sobol, the Commissioner of Education, appointed a committee composed mostly of minority persons (African Americans and Hispanics) to review New York State curricula. The committee had as its chief advisor the now notorious Professor Leonard Jeffries of the City College of New York, and it issued the famous (or infamous) report, "A Curriculum of Inclusion." The tone of this report can be accurately inferred from its opening sentence:

> African Americans, Asian Americans, Puerto Rican/Latinos, and Native Americans have all been the victims of an intellectual and educational oppression that has characterized the culture and institutions of the United States and the European American world for centuries. Negative characterizations and the absence of positive references have had a terribly damaging effect on the psyche of young people of African, Asian, Latino, and Native American descent.

The report was vigorously attacked. Perhaps the most effective attack was launched by the historian and education reformer

Diane Ravitch, who organized a group of historians to sign a statement condemning the report. The most prominent co-signer was Arthur Schlesinger, Jr. The Commissioner of Education then decided that he needed a second report and appointed a second committee. This time only half the members were minority; and the committee membership was divided between school teachers and administrators, on one hand, and academics on the other. I was on this committee, as was Arthur Schlesinger.

The committee produced another report, "One Nation, Many Peoples: A Declaration of Cultural Interdependence." That report also was attacked, most effectively by Arthur Schlesinger himself in his dissent to the report and in his book, *The Disuniting of America* (W.W. Norton, 1992), which he was writing while he served on the committee. Since then, the debate has continued, and it is very far from being over.

Almost everyone agrees that we need something more than a curriculum whose only objective is Americanization and assimilation; we need something that is more multicultural. Philosopher Charles Taylor, who perhaps is more sensitive to this issue because he teaches at McGill University in French-speaking Quebec, described multiculturalism as an expression of a "politics of recognition" (*Multiculturalism and "The Politics of Recognition,"* Princeton University Press, 1992). Racial and ethnic groups and women want to see themselves in the curriculum, included by both curriculum writers and teachers. Few attack this new thrust head-on. But what will this new emphasis on multiculturalism, on "recognition," do to American unity, to civic harmony, to the ability of minority students to learn and achieve? These are some of the key questions in the continuing debate over multiculturalism. I shall address five such questions in this paper.

Of course, I do not have the whole answer to any of them. It is easy enough to reject the extreme arguments on both sides. We are not going to base our elementary or secondary social studies education on some kind of fantasy about the role of Africa and blacks in world history. Africa is big and important, and blacks are part of the human race with all the virtues and defects of other humans. But there are certain things about which we can be quite clear. Whether or not some ancestral types of man first emerged in Africa has little bearing on subsequent human history; whether or not some kind of ur-language first emerged in Africa has little bearing on the subsequent history of language and literature. And whatever the achievements of Ancient Egypt, they have little connection with our world today or even with the world of the last thousand years. Whatever the scale of these achievements, persons of the black race could not have played more of a role in them than they do in the Egypt of today.

I realize that every one of these statements, and others I will make, may be disputed. Recently a student at Harvard asked me what could be done about the fact that Harvard students do not know that blacks discovered (or rather, "encountered") the New World long before Columbus. I could say only that I thought this supposed truth about early African sea voyages was highly unlikely, as unlikely as the notion that St. Brendan got here before Columbus. The idea of an African discovery of the New World probably plays the same role for some blacks that St. Brendan's mythical trip to the New World plays for some Irishmen. It is a poor substitute for worthier bases of self-esteem.

On the other hand, I do not quite join with the strongest critics of multiculturalism. I assume that there are some people in education who find the history and social studies of the 1940s, 1950s, and 1960s adequate to our circumstances and needs today. Undoubtedly there are some people who regret that today's high school history classes pay little attention to European history, compared to the history classes of the 1930s, when I took European history at James Monroe High School in the Bronx. Indeed, I do not believe that European history is taught any longer in the New York State high schools. It was replaced first by world history and then by "global studies," and so our high school students today will know nothing about the rise of the dynastic and absolute state in Europe, the war of the Spanish Succession, the rise of Prussia and Russia, the impact of the French Revolution, and a variety of other topics. I regret this because I like history (even when, or particularly when, it is completely irrelevant, such as the history of the Inca Empire). But I can make no argument on principled educational grounds that these and other topics should be restored. Similarly, I could have made no argument on principled educational grounds — despite my love for such antiquarian elements as the War of the Roses — that the history of England, which used to be taught in New England high schools at the turn of the century, should not be replaced by European history.

I believe that there are differences between these two unacceptable positions. For example, one extreme is based in large part on fantasy, while the other is based on nostalgia and a commitment to subjects that have lost significance for us in today's world.

Another difference is that a good part of the education that conservatives want to hold onto is indeed crucial to our world today. Our world has been shaped, and is being shaped, by science and technology in the area of the economy and by the power of the ideals of constitutionalism, democracy, and human rights in the area of politics. All of these ideas first established themselves in Europe, and they derive power in large part from the European expansion of the 15th to the 20th centuries, which spread European influences all over the world. Now origins — as I suggested in my comments on Egypt — do not make a prima facie case for inclusion in a curriculum, but these European origins are close to us chronologically and there is much we could not understand without European history. For example, we would be hard-pressed to understand the nature and problems of the Third World without this history.

Attitudes toward primacy of Europe may differ, but one cannot dispute that it is because of European ideas, power, and expansion that almost all modern states share similar ideals and similar approaches to realizing their ideals. Thus an emphasis on the primacy of Europe has a very different character from an emphasis on the primacy of Africa in defining and shaping our world.

But then, after the exercise of rejecting extremes, what are we to do about social studies education in the schools? Where along the spectrum from Afrocentrism to Eurocentrism do we pitch our tent? (And I realize that multiculturalism includes much more than Afrocentrism, but this dichotomy defines the heart of the controversy.) My approach to this question is to raise a series of subordinate questions, all of which are important in trying to define our stance on multiculturalism.

*1. Is truth the only test for a social studies curriculum?* "Teach the truth" would be an easy answer to our problem and is one that, in principle, both the extreme multiculturalists and their critics could accept. Indeed, both camps lay claim to the truth. The former say the truth has been ignored or worse, hidden, or even worse, stolen; and the achievements of the black race collectively or individual blacks have been attributed to Greeks or others.

The critics of multiculturalism also rest their case on "truth." But truth is a more difficult ground for the social studies today than it once was. In field after field today, so-called truths are challenged because they are based on doubtful assumptions or use flawed methodologies or reflect hidden prejudices. Mathematics and the sciences are relatively immune from this assault, although some radical sociologists of science have argued that even the truths of science are not wholly objective, not beyond the power of ordinary human interests and passions to shape them. But even these skeptical sociologists of science, I suspect, believe that the bridges over which they drive will hold in spite of the relative "truth" of various engineering principles.

However, in the other fields the assault on established doctrines, procedures, and findings is more serious. Few critics go to the extreme of saying that truth is simply what we prefer because of our own interests and what we then impose on others (or on society) because of our power to do so (although perhaps some deconstructionists may go that far). But it is clear today that just because most of the people working in an established discipline, using its accepted procedures and approaches, have come to certain conclusions, it does not mean that the rest of us have to believe the same things. "Truth" does not carry the weight it used to. Even those who argue against multicultural demands on the ground of historical truth recognize other grounds that may properly affect a curriculum. In the statement that Diane Ravitch and Arthur Schlesinger organized against the rather intemperate report, "A Curriculum of Inclusion," they asserted, among other things, that it would be *dangerous* "to use the school system to promote the division of our people into antagonistic racial groups." Presumably if certain truths had this effect, they would worry about emphasizing them.

No one really insists that truth is the only criterion for judging the social studies curriculum. After all, we have other objectives: those key objectives related to citizenship, the creation of national unity, the discouragement of group antagonism, and so on. If "truth" undermines these objectives — for example, by concentrating on the fact that the rich have more influence on public authorities than do the poor, or that there has been and is discrimination by one group against another, or that this kind of treatment could well justify hatred of one group for another or disrespect for public authority — then what?

Truth is an uncertain and incomplete guide. We do have other objectives in our social studies education in elementary and high schools. We used to tell the story of George Washington and the cherry tree. It was a way of teaching respect for honesty and for George Washington, the father of the country. But the story has been known to be a myth for a long time, probably as long as it has been told in schools. We now are told that we should tell other stories. But I assume that we are more willing to accept salutary myths in the elementary grades than in the high school. In the New York State curriculum, there is a section that refers to what we once knew as the Iroquois Federation (and now call the Hodenosaunee) and the influence of the knowledge of their federation on the framers of the Constitution. I believe, on the basis of assertions by authorities whom I have not studied in detail, that influence of the federation was insignificant, perhaps even nonexistent. How harmful is it that this assertion should be part of a curriculum? I believe that because of their educations, the framers of the Constitution were more likely influenced by their knowledge of federations in Classical Greece. How important is it that students should know that? If students believed that knowledge of the Hodenosaunee Federation influenced the framers and this belief raised Native Americans in the esteem of the fellow students, would that be a justification for teaching the story?

Recently there has been a controversy over the movie, *The Liberators,* and its central theme that black soldiers were among those who liberated the concentration camps. The movie is being presented as a way to improve relations between blacks and Jews. How seriously should we take the argument that the facts are not exactly as presented, that black soldiers were not among those who first reached the camps? The truth, the simple and unvarnished truth, may not be a sufficient guide. Certainly national unity and civic harmony also are objectives of our social studies teaching.

*2. What weight, then, do we give to national unity?* The great fear of the critics of multiculturalism is that a successful process of assimilation, or of integration, of the making of Americans with a common culture and a common loyalty, will be undermined by the stronger multicultural emphasis. Many of these critics have come through a school system — as I did myself — in which there simply was no acknowledgment of any culture other than the common culture and the common loyalty. I recall a description, often referred to in studies of Americanization, of a pageant in a Dearborn school in which diverse immigrants, each dressed in a distinctive costume, enter a huge melting pot on the school stage and emerge on the other side, all dressed alike. Certainly, that was the ambition of Americanization in the 1920s and 1930s. Not only were the history and culture of immigrants ignored, their day-to-day practices commonly were regarded as inferior and derided by teachers. It did not matter that one came from a home in which one traditionally had coffee and a roll for breakfast; one should have had orange juice and milk. There was no bilingualism; at best there was only the "steamer class" (an English immersion class) for rapid entry into regular classes.

Did this single-mindedness foster national unity? It certainly did not prevent the creation of a common American loyalty. Disloyalty was no problem even when we were fighting against the homelands of large numbers of immigrants. I believe that at one extreme it is this kind of fear about which we worry: disloyalty in war, divisiveness, the fear of becoming another Quebec, another Yugoslavia.

Therefore, aside from a concern for truth, there is a concern for national unity. But on this score a number of questions arise. How much national unity does the United States need? We have become more flexible about the matter. Perhaps we do not expect to fight any more world wars. Even if our relations with Japan worsen, we are more willing to accept — without attributions of disloyalty — the fact that Japanese Americans may look on Japan's economic success more kindly than other Americans do. Perhaps we exaggerated in those days of assimilation and Americanization how much national unity was necessary to fight foreign wars effectively. We certainly emphasized national unity much more during World War I than during World War II. Did it make our war efforts more successful in 1918?

Second, how confident are we that a curriculum that ignores or downplays differences produces a stronger loyalty than one that pays attention to differences? Perhaps in the popular culture of that bygone day, George M. Cohan songs and the like did more to create the common American culture than Americanization programs in schools. Today many aspects of the culture insist on and celebrate difference. How much do we know about the role of the public school in shaping a common identity or a common loyalty? What are the relative roles of the newspapers, radio, TV, movies, sports? I am reminded that parochial schools once were thought by many to promote disloyalty, or at least an alternative loyalty. We now think that the best patriots (even chauvinists) may come from parochial schools.

The relation between our efforts to create loyalty and unity through school curricula and the making of patriots is not simple. There is no necessary contradiction between an education that promotes a distinctive loyalty — different from national loyalty, as in the case of the parochial school — and a commitment to the interests of the nation and a willingness to participate in its defense. Of course, much depends on the character of that education. One can imagine a kind of multicultural education that would make children unwilling to serve in a national army or, indeed, in a local police force. But not only the formal education might lead to such a result; we must also consider the "education" provided by the media, by rap groups, by children's personal experiences with the government or the police.

I do not dismiss the fear that a necessary degree of national cohesiveness can be threatened by some kinds of multicultural education. But some of the dominant trends in multicultural education — for example, the trends that emphasize ethnic groups' contributions — should not have this effect. Indeed, such trends may actually strengthen national loyalty. If critics succeed, instead, in emphasizing oppression, discrimination, and grievance, then they could well undermine national unity. While the fear of diminished national cohesiveness is real and even reasonable, it also is perhaps exaggerated.

But the disunity about which we worry is not merely the disunity that undermines a national cohesiveness in the face of foreign or external threats. We also are concerned about the civic disharmony that may result from a multicultural emphasis. The fear of greater internal divisiveness — a Quebec or a Yugoslavia — is the issue here. For example, we have a long history of race riots. Does or could multicultural education promote the attitudes that make such unrest more likely? That is the basis of the third question.

*3. Does multiculturalism undermine civic harmony?* So much depends on the details: just what is in the curriculum, just how the teacher uses it. There is no question that an emphasis on oppression, discrimination, prejudice, and grievance would produce some disturbance of civic harmony. Yet the existence of discrimination and prejudice also is reality. The issue is one of balance and perspective. Before the New York State curriculum commit-tee, on which I served, I argued that the mistreatment of blacks, Mexican Americans, and others was part of American history and could not be ignored. But if one looked at the larger picture of U.S. history, one saw greater and greater inclusion, less and less discrimination, a steady increase in the protection of the rights of minorities, and constitutional protections and guarantees becom-ing increasingly effective.

A reputable scholar on the committee argued the opposite. He did not see the improvement or the changes that I saw. He could recognize some of the specifics that supported my argument — for example, that our immigration laws had abandoned racial re-strictions, that our civil rights had established nondiscrimination as the law of the land. But how firm, he asked, were these changes, how accepted? He pointed out that Haitians were not treated in immigration matters as well as Cubans and that blacks were still treated differently, according to current tests, in their efforts to get jobs or buy houses. I pointed to the protections of the Constitu-tion; he expressed fears that a white backlash would limit or over-turn these protections.

Our committee ended with the weak compromise that we should teach "multiple perspectives." Of course there are multi-ple perspectives in the social studies, but is that good enough? Are not some perspectives much better supported than others? I believe that some are, which brings us back to the argument for truth and all the problems that lie therein.

I would like to add to the claims that truth makes on the cur-riculum the claims of civic harmony. Would it be better for young blacks to believe that everyone is against them, that all their pro-tections are shams, that whites always will stop them from getting ahead, and that their oppression has scarcely been reduced since the days before the civil rights revolution and the Civil Rights Act? Or the reverse? Aside from that mass of evidence that sup-ports the reverse, perhaps the issue is a matter of practical utility. For their own good, their own progress, it would be better for blacks to believe that there has been improvement in their situation. It would be better for them to believe that the Ku Klux Klan and other anti-black groups are minuscule sects, rather than the wave of the future.

Unfortunately, some apocalyptic and paranoid beliefs are widespread among many of those who promote multiculturalism. After all, a substantial part of the black population believes that AIDS is a white plot against blacks. Spike Lee and Sister Souljah, who are perhaps among the most prominent and effective "teachers" of young blacks today, seem to believe this, or are willing to credit the story. So even if we thought it both true and better for minorities to believe in the ever-greater inclusiveness of American society, forces outside the public schools can, and often do, tell a different story.

I am afraid that many of education's critics do not believe that the ideal of civic harmony should be given primacy. A slogan prominently displayed following the Rodney King incident proclaimed, "No justice, no peace." How will we convince black Americans that a substantial measure of justice exists and that the sphere of justice is constantly expanding? And how do we get that story into a multicultural curriculum?

I come now to a quite different question but one of great importance in our consideration of citizenship. Judith Shklar, in her little book, *American Citizenship* (Harvard University Press, 1991), believes that full citizenship requires the ability to earn. I agree, and earnings depend on effective education. Proponents of multiculturalism claim that it will overcome the ineffectiveness of education for many minority children by enabling the minority child to see himself or herself in the curriculum. Thus we come to the fourth question.

*4. Does the student have to see himself in the curriculum if he is to learn effectively and to accept the authority of teacher and school?* The argument here is that when the student does not see members of his group among his teachers and administrators and in his textbooks, it all becomes foreign to him. (I am using "him" in the old-fashioned sense to refer to "her" also.) A related question is, Does the student have to have self-esteem to learn?

I believe that this question requires us to ask another, preliminary question: What do we mean by "self" in "self-esteem"? And what do we mean by "him" or "her" in the question, "Does the student have to see himself or herself in the teachers and the curriculum?" The assumption of the multiculturalist enthusiasts is that the "self" refers to the racial and ethnic self. But, of course, we are all made up of many selves. There is the self that prefers baseball to tennis, the self that prefers rock to classical music, the self that prefers social studies to science, the self that is poor rather than well-to-do, inner-city rather than suburban, Southern rather than Northern, Baptist rather than Lutheran, and so on. There are multiple selves, and not all can be represented in the teachers and the curriculum.

The assumption in multiculturalism is that of these many selves, one is dominant. Thus it is not necessary to represent the musical, athletic, regional, class, or religious self, because the racial or ethnic self is decisive. Because of this central role, if the racial or ethnic self is not represented, education cannot occur or is ineffective.

The answers I find (and use) to this argument are debaters' answers, which will not reach the core of this issue. One could say, for example, that the European immigrant child or the Asian child did not see himself in the curriculum or among teachers, and yet he or she learned what was necessary. If the white Protestants taught the Irish, and the Irish taught the Jews and Italians, and the Jews and the Italians teach the blacks and Hispanics, why is there a problem in the last term of this progression, where there was not in the former? One response would be that none of the learning of this type was effective, and the matter is the same (or, for other reasons, worse) today.

Another debater's answer: Not everyone can be represented in the curriculum or in the teaching staff because there are scores of ethnic and racial groups today in every big city. Therefore, specific representation of every ethic or racial type is an unrealistic and impossible demand. The response from the multiculturalists could be that, although it may be unrealistic for all to be represented, it is possible to represent the two largest ethnic groups in our city schools, blacks and Hispanics. After all, it is their academic deficiency, particularly of blacks, that is an important initiating cause of the debate.

I once wrote that those educated in the heyday of Americanization said, "We didn't need it, why do they? We didn't want it, why do they?" But I have come, albeit reluctantly, to the conclusion that the position of blacks (and perhaps Hispanics, although here I would still resist the conclusion) is different from that of earlier immigrants in several radical ways. While one can dispute the need for either the old immigrants or the new immigrants to "see themselves in the curriculum," perhaps for blacks it is different.

At one time black leaders believed that it was not different for blacks. They wanted for blacks exactly what existed for whites. They hoped for assimilation in all respects into American society, culture, economy, and polity. That was the aim of school desegregation. But that attitude began to change in the late 1960s, and now I wonder if anyone believes in that assimilationist ideal today. What is needed in education depends on the values, ideals, and conceptions that students bring to school. If a student's ideal is "to become an American," the fact that the culture of the student's group and family is ignored or even derided may have no serious negative effect. Many immigrants come to the United States to become Americans, to be Americanized. Perhaps most of the Hispanic or Asian immigrants arrive today with the same hope and intention. But the great majority of blacks are not immigrants.

Groups can define themselves in various ways, and they have some degree of freedom in defining themselves. At one point blacks did define themselves simply as struggling for the same place in American society, achieved by the same means. That is what I mean by the assimilationist ideal. Today, many blacks define themselves differently. Not to see themselves in the faculty, in the administrators, or in the curriculum equates to imposed inferiority. The counter-arguments we could make — you don't see black teachers because many blacks are no longer interested in becoming teachers or cannot pass the tests, or the place of blacks in the curriculum is the one that scholarly investigation properly has determined it should be — just will not wash for many black Americans.

Groups define themselves — nations define themselves — quite independently from how scholars believe that history and experience have defined them. Their self-definition is a reflection of their perceived reality and an expression of will. A good deal of myth and half-truth infuse these self-definitions, as we know from the history of nationalism. But a new process of self-definition is occurring among black Americans, I believe. Perhaps I am too impressed by the more militant leaders and group advocates. But it seems that a range of approaches, some very different from multiculturalism, will be proposed by black educators and will work in some exclusively or predominately black schools. Some such schools do emphasize Shakespeare or mathematics instead of black studies, and their programs work successfully. But many do not. I would prefer Shakespeare and mathematics for black students — I think it would do them and the nation more good — but the decision is not going to be mine.

I would hope that the trends that seem to be making multiculturalism powerful in schools and districts with large black enrollments do not take hold among Hispanics. But they are already very strong among that group, too, particularly because of the shared Spanish language. I hope this trend does not take hold among Asian Americans, who are the most rapidly growing group in our country. Many Hispanics and Asian Americans have a real choice: the immigrant path or the minority path; the story that emphasizes achievement and upward progress or the story that emphasizes oppression, discrimination, and prejudice; the story that emphasizes assimilation, acculturation, or integration or the story that encourages separateness. A multicultural emphasis does not inevitably mean an emphasis on repression history and separatism as a response to it. But many trends within multiculturalism do encourage these emphases.

5. *Finally, how much does the battle over the social studies curriculum matter?* The battle over the curriculum is most promi-

nent in the social studies and the humanities. It really cannot get much of a hold in mathematics or science. In those fields, no one asks who invented what, and it doesn't matter. The issue is, can you solve the problem, do you know how to get to an answer, is this the reason the experiment works? In these fields, there is a true objectivity. A formula or an equation either works or does not work. It is true, or it is false.

In the course of the debates over multiculturalism in the New York State curriculum committee to which I have referred, I had to ponder our final report and consider whether I should sign it. The report endorsed "multiple perspectives." I wondered why the debates in the committee had been mostly among the members who came from universities, while the teachers and administrators seemed to accept without any question the multicultural thrust, or at least they did not dispute it. I asked a school administrator why this was so, and he said, "I don't care how they learn to read and write."

But I believe that these skills — reading and writing, calculating, being able to perform in mathematics and science — are, in the end, the most important elements of education. If a certain thrust in how we teach the humanities and the social sciences is associated with overall greater success in these crucial skills and capacities — and we do not yet know that it is — then is that not a powerful argument?

In our inner cities, our schools are predominately minority, black and Hispanic. There are integrated schools, of course; but more integrated schools are to be found in our suburbs and smaller towns. In the big city schools where substantial percentages of teachers and administrators are from racial or ethnic minorities, the top administrators almost always are minority. Suppose these teachers and administrators conclude that a stronger multicultural emphasis helps to involve students more in their studies, what position can the critics of multiculturalism take?

I am impressed that in numerous accounts of experimental programs, teachers of various ethnic and racial backgrounds seem to adopt the multicultural thrust, seem to think that it helps and that it involves the students more than a classical or traditional (or more distant) subject matter might involve them in learning. This is not a universal experience, of course; but it seems to be a common one. That was not my experience as a student, nor was it the experience of most of my contemporaries. We would have found learning Yiddish poets instead of Keats and Wordsworth, Jewish history instead of European history, the story of American Jewish contributions rather than the story of colonization either boring or demeaning or embarrassing. That was undoubtedly in part because we attributed more prestige to the education we thought of as classical or traditional or American than to our own personal experiences. But I have the strong impression that things have changed radically, and it is easier to reach the inner-city minority student today through his or her personal experience, the experiences and background of his or her distinctive group, rather than through a curriculum that ignores that group.

One sees little in the education journals critical of multiculturalism, while I see endless material on how to implement multicultural education. Running a search in ERIC on materials on multiculturalism over a recent period, I found hundreds of items applauding or implementing multiculturalism and only one item that was critical. The discussion in the education journals is very different from the discussion to be found in the mass media, where the criticism of multiculturalism is dominant.

What does this tell us? One conclusion might be that educators are pusillanimous, overly influenced by multicultural enthusiasts and militants, perhaps intellectually incapable of resisting their demands. On the other hand, it may tell us that, on the ground, in classrooms where teachers are engaged in working with students from many racial and ethnic backgrounds, they see a necessity for something different. Even if we do not have enough experience to know whether the multicultural approach is better, teachers believe that it will be more effective in helping inner-city students to the real ends of education in the elementary and secondary grades, to acquiring the essential skills and tools of learning. Because of this possibility, one must, even while fighting multicultural excesses, acknowledge the possibility that multicultural approaches are one way to educational achievement for our inner-city minority children.

If this is the case, then multicultural approaches to education also offer one route to more effective citizenship, for that depends, first of all, on participation in the society, the economy, and the culture. I am willing to risk more severe arguments, controversies, and debates on multiculturalism, if one result is to involve our minority students more deeply in their education. Whether that end will be achieved is something we don't know yet. But the possibility should lead us to take the multicultural argument seriously and to give it some credit.

# Plurality, Diversity, and the Public Space

## BY MAXINE GREENE

To speak of plurality, as Hannah Arendt did, is to speak of human beings in their distinctiveness (Arendt 1958, pp. 175-78). No one can be considered identical with any other, no matter the degree of gender, class, ethnic, or cultural identity ostensibly shared. No one can be conceived of as an endlessly reproducible repetition of the same model, to be understood in accord with general laws of behavior. Nor can any human being be predefined. The self is not something ready-made, John Dewey wrote, "but something in continuous formation through choice of action" (Dewey 1916, p. 408).

There is no way, said Arendt, "to solidify in words the living essence of the person as it shows itself in the flux of action and speech" (1958, p. 10). Within that flux, the person is forever embarking on new beginnings, reaching beyond what is to what might be. Only when viewed from without or from the vantage point of an institution or a system does her or his movement seem susceptible to plotting, prediction, and quantifying. From the situated perspective of the actor or the agent, the one charting a path in the midst of things, there always are diverging roads. In the Robert Frost poem, they appear to diverge "from where I stood"; it was not a view from nowhere that captured them as divergent. And from the viewpoint of the poet (or the seeker or the teacher), there can be no knowing where either road will end.

One way of beginning an examination of pluralism and multiculturalism is with a vision of what it is to be human. Here the existing person, of whatever age, is viewed as involved in "we-relations" (Schutz 1964, p. 38) and at once distinctive, always in process of self-definition in an intersubjective world. We think in terms of education, not mere skill training, largely because of the capacity to seek intentionally. Wherever we are trying to build a democratic community, we cannot settle for conditioning or merely imposing uniform behaviors from without. Nor can we ascribe fixed essences to people or treat them as "representative" of given groups, cultures, or even genders. Treating them as various and situated, we have to take into account a diversity of perspectives and realities. "The hallmark of modern consciousness," writes Clifford Geertz, "is its enormous multiplicity." The problem of cultural integration for him is one "of making it possible for people inhabiting different worlds to have a genuine and reciprocal impact upon one another" (Geertz 1983, p. 161). If we are not to suffer "the interplay of a disorderly crowd of not wholly commensurable visions," we must create conditions that allow some "reciprocal impact." So it may be when we think of educating for the emergence of a public space.

For Arendt, such a space is created when people come together in speech and action and try to bring into existence an "in-between" among themselves. The reader is moved to summon up images of spaces where diverse people recognize and relate to one another; indeed, where they take responsibility because they are recognized not as data or alien beings or cases, but as persons choosing for themselves what they might be or want to be or think they should turn out to be. What is evoked is an atmosphere of movement, of undertakings and renewals. There is dialogue, a sense of heteroglossia (Bakhtin 1981, p. 331), which is something other than speechlessness, stasis, and passivity.

As with Dewey's conception of a public, the appearance of shared interests is highlighted; persons from their diverse locations work for concern. For Dewey, a public begins to come into existence when various people begin paying heed to the consequences of certain private transactions — consequences that affect the lives of people outside the sphere of those transactions (Dewey 1954, pp. 13-14). When there is reflection on those events, when groups of persons begin to appreciate and to care about what is happening (as they sometimes do with respect to the plight of abused children, homeless families, undocumented immigrants, or poorly served students), then they are likely to open a public space in which demands on representatives can be made and people can begin to find their voices and to express what they think and feel.

Although Dewey and his contemporaries were aware of different "associated groups," they were not likely to take into account gender difference or cultural diversity or even class divisions as factors relevant to education and public life. "Persons," even "individuals" tended to imply something generalized, even universal, despite the acknowledgment that selves were not ready-made. They were, as Toni Morrison puts it, "non-racialized" (1992, p. 16). Their diverse cultural experiences (as Irish or Jewish immigrants, say, or as immigrants from the South or Mennonites from the Rhineland) and their sharply differentiated experiences because of gender difference were rarely taken into account. In the 19th century, novelists and poets were far more likely to take note of what Walt Whitman called "the many long dumb voices . . . the forbidden voices" (1931, p. 53).

In Herman Melville's *Moby Dick*, the *Pequod*'s crew is made up largely of Islanders,

> each *Isolato* living on a separate continent of his own. Yet now, federated along one keel, what a set these Isolatoes were! An Anacharsis Clootz deputation from all the isles of the sea, and all the ends of the earth, accompanying Old Ahab in the *Pequod* to lay the world's grievances before that bar from which not very many of them ever come back. Black Little Pip — he never did — oh, no! he went before. Poor Alabama boy! On the grim *Pequod*'s forecastle, ye shall ere long see him, beating on his tambourine; prelusive of the eternal time, when sent for, to the great quarter-deck on high, he was bid strike in with angels, and beat his tambourine in glory; called a coward here, hailed a hero there! (Melville 1981, p. 123)

Who at that time paid humane, nonphilanthropic heed to little Pip? Who would take note of "pagan harpooners"? And who would think of sharing a bed with strange, tattooed Queequeg, discovering him as a fellow man and sharing a bed with him, making "a cozy, loving pair?"

In Mark Twain's *The Adventures of Huckleberry Finn*, for all the innocence of Huck's vernacular speech and all the ironies, the distinctiveness of Jim's voice and the growth of his wisdom become increasingly clear, especially as the raft moves closer and closer to freedom. There is no way to say "mankind" without recognizing Jim's exclusion; the very noun "man" becomes a fearfully insufficient construct, as we experience Jim's striving to be. Granted, the novel was written by a white man for white readers; relatively few African Americans had opportunities (or the recognition required) to write and speak for themselves. But the heeding is there, as is the care, in spite of Southern contexts. Most often it took women to do as much for women. And slowly they did so: Louisa May Alcott, Charlotte Gilman, Kate Chopin, Rebecca Harding Davis, and a very few others began publishing, articulating the differences more than the similarities between men and women, separated by hierarchy and patriarchy as they were. We need but think of the "yellow wallpaper" (Gilman 1973), of Edna's "awakening" (Chopin 1972), of Jo March's divided self (Alcott 1936) to be reminded that the artists saw early on what was generally thrust out of sight.

It should have been clearer, when the new century began, that attacks on the familiar were multiplying and that an "irruption of otherness" (Clifford 1988, p. 13) was in the making. There were the laborers and immigrants in the classes at Hull House; there were the faces of the poor captured by Jacob Riis in New York; there were the Eastern Europeans coming in their masses for the first time, often embarrassing earlier arrivals. There were the Chinese railway workers carelessly thrust into invisibility by the Exclusion Laws and petty, brutal prohibitions only recently brought to our attention by novels such as Maxine Hong Kingston's *China Men* (1989). For all the seismic changes, however, changes that only occasionally broke through the presumably smooth surfaces, fictions of uniformity and harmony were maintained.

E.L. Doctorow captures them when he describes the "reality" of life in 1906 in *Ragtime*.

> Teddy Roosevelt was President. The population customarily gathered in great numbers either out of doors for parades, public concerts, fish fries, political picnics, social outings, or indoors in meeting halls, vaudeville theatres, operas, ballrooms. There seemed to be no entertainment that did not involve great swarms of people. Trains and steamers and trolleys moved them from one place to another. That was the style, that was the way people lived. Women were stouter then. They visited the fleet carrying white parasols. Everyone wore white in summer. Tennis racquets were hefty and the racquet faces elliptical. There was a lot of sexual fainting. There were no Negroes. There were no immigrants. (Doctorow 1975, pp. 3-4)

In the framework of the novel, it takes the anarchist Emma Goldman to convince Evelyn Nesbit that, at least, there were Negroes and immigrants as well.

"That was the way people lived": Doctorow is evoking an official story that still summons up notions of melting pot and social balance wheel, for all that it excludes. The book deals, of course, with the humiliation and obliteration of a decent, proud black man who is simply not permitted to belong or to become. Today, with the advent of multicultural talk, it has become difficult to maintain the pretenses of a peaceful homogeneity or of "public concerts" that drown out discordant voices. We are being asked to come to terms with a heterogeneity and a multilinguality generally unacknowledged except in the realms of the arts. We are being asked, as well, to confront the meanings of contingency, or the dependence of perspective and point of view on lived situations or locations in a fragmented world. We are being asked to reconcile this contingency view with a recognition of the need to construct a "great community" out of which (as Dewey wrote) "an organized, articulate Public" might emerge. He emphasized, it will be recalled, the wedding of "free social inquiry" to "the art of full and moving communication"; and there are few thinkers today who would ignore the centrality of significant discourse, of dialogue, of speech. Nor would they ignore the necessity for reflectiveness, not only with regard to what is valued and held in common, but with regard to the very nature of the connections that hold people together in diverse "webs of relationship" (Arendt 1958, p. 182).

The difference — in the contemporary winds of multiplicity and change — has partly to do with how the "great community" now is to be conceived and how "the art of full and moving communication" is to be defined. In an earlier time, the model for community-building could be found in the New England town meeting, where the male members of the township (including those who were relative newcomers) could resolve conflicts, decide on necessary projects, and contain whatever disagreements arose. With the growth of cities and the rise in immigration, models might be found in local wards, even in school boards, in which the Italians or the Irish or the Poles or the Jews might work together on their special interests and the connection between those interests and what they discovered as they moved out into the surrounding society.

It is probably important to realize at this point in the century that the visible "players" in economic and political life, those moving to share in the structures of power, were primarily (although not always) male and almost without exception European in origin. Returning to Doctorow, we might reiterate that "there were immigrants"; but, in spite of the work of people such as W.E.B. Du Bois (1982), and in spite of the Harlem Renaissance, African Americans achieved an irresistible presence only with the Civil Rights movement in the 1960s. Women, long silenced even in the midst of their struggles for equality, began making their "different" voices (Gilligan 1982) audible almost two decades later. Even today, there is the most gradual recognition of the ways in which maternal thinking and relational thinking might enrich and enhance the "full and moving communication" so essential for a public space.

Dewey was indeed aware of the importance of what we now call "situated" knowing and associate with what have been mainly women's experiences. In his *Art as Experience*, he wrote of mind as a verb, as "care in the sense of solicitude, anxiety, as well as of active looking after things that need to be tended." He said that it denoted all the ways "in which we deal consciously and expressly with the situations in which we find ourselves"; and he rejected all treatments of the mind as an independent entity "which attends, purposes, cares, notices, and remembers," all notions of the mind as an isolated being (Dewey 1931, p. 263). Nevertheless, concerned as he was with "communion" and "consensus," he did not open the way for the heteroglossia many now believe may make the public sphere richer, potentially resonant with multiple voices.

In part, this may be because of his proposal that "social inquiry" be wedded to "the art of full and moving communication." Granting his interest in imagination, in qualitative thinking, conceivably his focus on intelligent and hypothetical approaches to problems kept him from confronting some of the implications of the embodied, engaged, related modes of knowing that could not but challenge the patriarchal mode. There remain, most of us realize, untapped perspectives on we-relationships and what it signifies to be together — perspectives, "provinces of meaning" that the more pluralist William James could summon up, areas of difference that may not have seemed reconcilable with a Deweyan conception of community.

We might consider, for instance, the very recent acknowledgment of Hispanic and Latino traditions, the surprised awe in the face of Colombian novels and Mexican portraits, the recognition of the expanding significance of Borges' *Ficciones* (1962), of Fuentes' inclusive points of view. Frida Kahlo, Gabriel García Márquez, Oscar Hijuelos: all such newly found artists do not subvert what we call our canon; nor need their visions eat away at what exists as our public space. They offer alternative ways of seeing and saying. At once they make possible more sensitive modes of attending to young persons creating themselves out of memories and images somewhat different from ours, but demanding recognition and regard.

There are examples, many examples, of contingency in literature — or the ways in which appreciation and even "background knowledge" are functions of experience. Jamaica Kincaid, for instance, tells (in *Lucy*) of a young woman who has come from Antigua to work as an "au pair girl" in New York. When her employer delightedly invites her one day to see the springtime daffodils in Central Park, Lucy abruptly recalls what it was like for her to memorize and recite a poem about daffodils by a dead white British poet when she attended the Queen Victoria Middle School at home. Very conscious of being looked at as a colonized person, she ponders her two-facedness:

> Outside, I seemed one way; inside, I was another; outside false, inside true. And so I made pleasant little noises that showed both modesty and appreciation, but inside I was making a vow to erase from my mind, line by line, every word of that poem. (Kincaid 1990, p. 18)

Later, confronted by yellow flowers in New York, she wants to cut them down with a scythe. Her desire might well strike a teacher (or a Wordsworth lover) as trivial, if not absurd; but surely no judgment of incorrectness can be validated, simply because "sorrow and bitterness" surged up in her at the very thought of the poem. Surely, this does not imply that "To a Daffodil" ought to be excised from the literary canon. It simply means that there are more interpretations than we can guess, that other visions might well enrich and complicate the poem.

A different insight is to be found in Toni Morrison's *The Bluest Eye* (1972), perhaps one even more important because it has to do with the "official story" or a meta-narrative of our culture indirectly suggested by E.L. Doctorow. It may be recalled how an "official story" is embodied in the first paragraph of the well-known basal reader, *Dick and Jane*. That paragraph is presented at the start of *The Bluest Eye* in three typographies, the last one so run together that it serves as a kind of background, or "white noise"; and the reader is made abruptly aware of how that primer deformed the realities of children who did not live in houses with white fences, did not have loving fathers with jobs, or did not have attentive mothers who stayed home all day. Pecola Breedlove here is black, poor, unloved, and wholly convinced she is hopelessly ugly. She wants, above all else, to have blue eyes and to look like Shirley Temple. Only then will she be seen to be an appealing, lovable human child.

Pecola is driven mad by that as much as by the rape she suffers at the hands of her own desperate father. Most of her story, however, is told by Claudia, another poor black girl who happens to come from a concerned, gruffly loving home. She is able to refuse the terrible objectness of Shirley Temple dolls and images. She also is able to give her own experiences meaning that Pecola's never had by telling the story, her story and Pecola's. At the beginning, initiating a flashback tale, Claudia tells of Pecola's pregnancy and the death of her baby; she says that here innocence and faith were no more productive than Pecola's father's lust or despair.

> What is clean now is that of all that hope, fear, lust, love, and grief, nothing remains but Pecola and the unyielding earth. Cholly Breedlove is dead; our innocence too. The seeds shriveled and died; her baby too. There is really nothing more to say — except why. But since why is difficult to handle, one must take refuge in how. (p. 160)

Perhaps oddly, in Tillie Olsen's "I Stand Here Ironing," there is a similar reference to Shirley Temple, this one in connection with the narrator's daughter, a child of "depression, war, and fear." Midway through the story the mother recalls the child fretting over her appearance, "thin and dark and foreign-looking at a time when every little girl was supposed to look or thought she should look like a chubby blonde replica of Shirley Temple." At the end, when the mother sums it up and finds she cannot "total" all that happened, she thinks again that her daughter "was dark and thin and foreign-looking in a world where the prestige went to blondness and curly hair and dimples, she was slow where glibness was prized." It takes time to realize and to articulate the damage done by the culture's fixities and icons; and it is not surprising that this should have been pointed out by women made abruptly aware of what voicelessness and subordination had done when it came to their becoming. Without words, many had no means of finding out, as the mother says in Olsen's story, that they are more than dresses on the ironing board, "helpless before the iron." This connects with what the same Tillie Olsen wrote in one of the essays in her *Silences*. Writing about the suppressed voices in our history, she said that silence represents "an unnatural thwarting of what struggles into being, but cannot" (Olsen 1983, p. 6).

Clearly, there is a connection between overcoming the silences and releasing persons — excluded, disqualified persons — to struggle into being, to become, to choose themselves. And this, in turn, underlines the feminist attentiveness to story-telling and the growing interest in narrative as a way of endowing experience with meaning. Jerome Bruner has written about story-telling as a mode of thought that is as significant as the logical linguistic mode (Bruner 1986, pp. 11-12). Stories, he reminds us, deal with two "realities": the psychic reality of Lucy, say, remembering her New York place, or of Pecola, conscious of being hopelessly alone in the world; and the surrounding reality at the horizon of their attention. This might include the ongoing landscape of Antigua or "the land of the entire country" that Morrison's Claudia says "was hostile to marigolds that year." If we can empower young people and move them to shape their stories and to tell them, to present something of their realities in an open space, then we also may provoke them to pose the questions in which learning always begins.

In this case, they might be questions about the world that continues, admittedly or not, to colonize young women like Lucy or (just as harmfully) to cast them as exotics. The questions might be about how young people can be so damaged when poverty presses down on their parents, or the questions might be about what can be done to fertilize the ground so that, indeed, more marigolds will grow. Philosopher Charles Taylor writes that "because we cannot but orient ourselves to the good, and thus determine our place relative to it and hence determine the direction of our lives, we must inescapably understand our lives in narrative form, as a 'quest'" (Taylor 1989, pp. 51-52). This is another argument for the encouragement of story-writing and story-telling, not only on the part of learners but on the part of teachers willing to share their own struggles for direction and to communicate some sense of shared becoming among persons striving for recognition, reaching out to be.

Engaging with works of fiction — children's literature, adult novels and stories — can contribute to the shaping of experience in the form of story. There is great interest today in approaches to reading that encourage the participation of readers in the production of meanings, rather than the unearthing of hidden meanings in texts. Encountering *The Bluest Eye*, for example, we have learned that we can enter it against the background of our own lives, look through the perspectives those lives make available, even as we look through those provided by Claudia, Frida, Mrs. Breedlove, Cholly Breedlove, Pecola Breedlove, and the other characters, not to mention the narrator or narrators or the persona emergent from the social reality of Toni Morrison herself. Attempting to integrate those perspectives, many of which are dissonant with one another, we have to use our imaginations to create connections, to achieve the book as meaningful. We must, as Jean-Paul Sartre has said, lend the book our lives (1949, p. 45). The meanings we produce in so doing bring to light relations, patterns, and connections in our experience; we see more; we advance somehow in our quests. Michael Fischer has written that the kind of participation just described eventually may activate in readers the desire for *communitas* with others, "while preserving rather than effacing differences" (Fischer 1986, p. 233). This is the point — or ought to be the point — of schoolwork that is oriented to diversity.

If it is indeed the case that engagement with works of literature may release persons to find more meaning in their lives, we can realize anew the value of diversifying the works we make available. Antiguans such as Lucy do not have to be confined to Caribbean poetry and fiction; but it seems likely that an encounter early on with Derek Walcott's poetry might stimulate her self-reflection and provoke her own questioning more fruitfully than an alienating introduction to Wordsworth. A growing acquaintance on the part of American educators with Walcott's work (which never would have been included in the canon a quarter-century ago) can only expand horizons, move student readers, to use Walcott's phrase, "beyond insularity" (1987, p. 79). Or perhaps Lucy, still uncertain of her worth as a young woman, might be aroused subtly and profoundly by a woman writer, such as Isabel Allende, Michelle Clift, Clarise Lispector, Marguerite Duras, Alice Walker, Jane Smiley, each of whose mode of being might make her feel more recognized, more at home in the world.

The point is that if Lucy is encouraged to choose herself on her own informed initiative, Caribbean art works and women's literature might offer her the most appropriate materials with which to begin shaping an authentic self. Restless and defiant as she is, she cannot detach herself wholly from her culture or change her gender or her class origin. They are part of her condition, but she is not entirely conditioned by them. The more she is enabled to name them, to become critically conscious of them, the more she will realize that she is not living inside a container. There are gaps; there are spaces. The more she recognizes the meanings in origins and context, the more she will see that their significance for her depends a great deal on the interpretations she makes in dialogues and collaborative activities undertaken with others like her — and some unlike her, with teachers, with the adults she meets along her way.

It seems at least likely that teachers attending to what is said and done within their diverse classrooms may perceive alternative possibilities of life and thought for themselves. They might, as they encourage their students to do, not only engage in "social inquiry" to make sense of what often appears to be an unrecognizable world (with dissonant new music blaring in the background, kaleidoscopic fabricated images obscuring the printed pages of books). They also might explore the power of the cognitive capacity called imagination to break through what is taken for granted, to loosen what Dewey called the "crust" of conformity. Cynthia Ozick, aware of distances and the wonder of metaphors, writes about the ways in which metaphor presses on language and story-telling, inhabiting language at its most concrete. She talks about its use in coming in touch with dead writers, who are in so many ways, "that which we know" (yes, Melville, for instance, even Wordsworth and Cervantes and Omar Khayyam, if only we can cross the distances and imagine). Ozick concludes:

> Through metaphor, the past has the capacity to imagine us, and we it. Through metaphorical concentration, doctors can imagine what it is to be their patients. Those who have no pain can imagine those who suffer. Those at the center can imagine what it is to be outside. The strong can imagine the weak. Illuminated lives can imagine the dark. Poets in their twilight can imagine the borders to stellar fire. We strangers can imagine the familiar hearts of strangers. (1989, p. 283)

We want to be concerned not only about strangers in their unfamiliarity; we want to be attentive to their pain, to their dignity. We want, as Michael Ignatieff says, to be attentive to "the needs of strangers" (1984). However, even as we strive for attentiveness, we cannot make the assumption that we know better what other human beings need than they know themselves. Part of our work in education and politics is to devise situations in which people can become articulate about what they desire and need (beyond elemental necessities, which ought to be guaranteed). Cornel West draws to our attention the fact that black cultural practices (as seen in popular culture, sports, church services, jazz):

> emerge out of a reality they cannot not know — the ragged edges of the real, of necessity; a reality historically constructed by white supremacist practices in North America during the age of Europe. These ragged edges — of not

being able to eat, not to have shelter, not to have health care — all this is infused into the strategies and styles of black cultural practices. (West 1989, p. 23)

He realizes that all people have suffered social misery, but he chooses to make the point that African Americans have suffered it "in the midst of the most prosperous and wealthy country in the world." We also are being reminded, as by Toni Morrison, that ours was the country capable of creating free institutions even while writing laws protecting slavery. Morrison insists, as well, that nothing highlighted our freedom more than slavery. It made it possible to project a "not-me," an Africanism that was "a fabricated brew of darkness, otherness, alarm, and desire that is uniquely American." Whether we find this convincing or not, it suggests that self-reflective examination is necessary if white people are to clarify their own "mute, meaningless, . . . veiled, curtained . . . Whiteness" (Morrison 1992, p. 45). By doing so, she says, we might have a better chance of surviving as persons and as members of a community-in-the-making in an agonized, inchoate world. Again, it would appear, we have a better opportunity to achieve some kind of mutuality in our plurality if we can tap imaginatively into lives captured in story and in literary art, if we can recognize a role for situated knowing and situated speaking and pay heed to vantage points denied for too long.

This may become an instance of the shared concern around which and from which a public might emerge. The concern may have largely to do with inventing situations in which the long-silenced, those at "the ragged edge of the real," are provided opportunities not only to speak for themselves and what they need, but to demand representation that will support their rights to mend the ragged edges, to repair the flaws in some manner, in other words, to transform. We and those we teach must have opportunities to make "different" experiences objects of our experience as we open texts — diverse texts, telling stories hitherto unknown and telling them well — and try to recognize what we have pushed aside. Opening spaces in our classrooms that enable all kinds of persons to appear before one another articulating the nature of their searches, we have to make available works that legitimize ways of being once disqualified, too long scorned: works by women, works by the newcomers streaming into this country, works by artists and writers displaying their own visions of what Dostoyevsky knew, and Flaubert, and Kant, and the Brontes, and the poet Elizabeth Bishop (in Brazil for 17 years and home again).

Not to be forgotten is the desire to go beyond, if the circumstances allow. We might be reminded of Ntozake Shange's *Lady in Brown*, recalling what it was like as a child in the St. Louis Library, running (without permission) into the Adult Reading Room, because she had grown beyond Winnie the Pooh and Pippi Longstocking (Shange 1977, pp. 25-26). We might recall the young James Baldwin devouring Dostoyevsky or Virginia Woolf, desperate to move beyond the confines and move into the university library, where women were not allowed.

Sartre, who believed that we are all characterized by going beyond situations and by what we succeed at making of what we have been through, thought that "going beyond" is a need at the root of the human situation. Going beyond has to do with bringing something into being, what Sartre called a "project." Starting with that project, he wrote, we try to negate what we cannot use and at once move to what has not yet been:

> A flight and a leap ahead, at once a refusal and a realization, the project retains and unveils the surpassed reality which is refused by the very movement which surpassed it. This knowing is a moment of praxis. (Sartre 1963, p. 92)

Of course, we do not know with any certainty. In a culture still distrustful of the life of the mind, with young people's peer groups satisfied to live in their own enclosed worlds, with persisting poverty and hopelessness exacerbating the estrangement of minority groups from one another, we know that education can only launch tentative new initiatives in domains still poorly understood. But if indeed the consequences of what has been happening cluster around the voicelessness and resentful powerlessness of thousands and thousands of young today, to care about such consequences finally may mean to take pedagogical action. And pedagogical action is the kind of action that qualifies the disqualified, empowers them to embark on their own beginnings, to devise their own projects, to refuse and to realize, and to surpass.

In Arendt's image of the public space, there are stories, too; there are persons speaking directly to one another and weaving webs of relationship out of an intangible "subjective in-between." The realm of human affairs, says Arendt, consists of that web of relationships. The "agent" who is revealed through authentic speech always becomes part of an existing web where the consequences of her or his actions can be felt. The "who" that is revealed, she writes, and the occurrence of a new beginning "start a new process which eventually emerges as the unique life story of the newcomer, affecting uniquely the life stories of all those with whom s/he comes in contact" (Arendt 1958, p. 184). She affirms, however, that although we are all in some way the heroes, the agents of those stories, the stories become part of the flow of the culture's story; and we are never the authors or the producers of their outcomes. The outcomes are always open; always there are untapped possibilities.

A community, a democratic community, said Dewey, always is in the making. Arendt would add that there always are newcomers, always new stories feeding into living history out of which community emerges and is continually renewed. We may in time create a public space that can contain differences and that will allow for changing patterns of reciprocity. It is a matter of recognition; it is a matter of imagination. It is a matter of choosing to act on what humiliates and brings pain. It is a matter of reaffirming democratic principles and choosing to live in accord with them "as if" they were grounded in something objective. This has been in no way an argument for relativism or for empty inclusion. It has been an argument for openings and reciprocity, an argument for the remaking of a many-faceted community that may attain a coherence, a majesty, and a passion of which we still have no idea.

# References

Alcott, L.M. *Little Women*. Boston: Little, Brown, 1936.

Arendt, H. *The Human Condition*. Chicago: University of Chicago Press, 1958.

Bakhtin, M. *The Dialogic Imagination*. Austin: University of Texas Press, 1981.

Borges, J.L. *Ficciones*. New York: Grove Press, 1962.

Bruner, J. *Actual Minds, Possible Worlds*. Cambridge, Mass.: Harvard University Press, 1986.

Chopin, K. *The Awakening*. New York: Avon, 1972.

Clifford, J. *The Predicament of Culture*. Cambridge, Mass.: Harvard University Press, 1988.

Dewey, J. *Art as Experience*. New York: Minton, Balch and Co., 1931.

Dewey, J. *Democracy and Education*. New York: Macmillan, 1916.

Dewey, J. *The Public and Its Problems*. Athens, Ohio: Swallow Press, 1954.

Doctorow, E.L. *Ragtime*. New York: Random House, 1975.

Du Bois, W.E.B. *The Souls of Black Folk*. New York: New American Library, 1982.

Fischer, M.J. "Ethnicity and the Arts of Memory." In *Writing Culture*, edited by J. Clifford and G.E. Marcus. Berkeley: University of California Press, 1986.

Geertz, C. *Local Knowledge*. New York: Basic Books, 1983.

Gilligan, C. *In a Different Voice*. Cambridge, Mass.: Harvard University Press, 1982.

Gilman, C.P. *The Yellow Wallpaper*. New York: Feminist Press, 1973.

Ignatieff, M. *The Needs of Strangers*. London: Hogarth Press, 1984.

Kincaid, J. *Lucy*. New York: Farrar, Straus, & Giroux, 1990.

Kingston, M.H. *China Men*. New York: Vintage, 1989.

Melville, H. *Moby Dick*. Berkeley: University of California Press, 1981.

Morrison, T. *The Bluest Eye*. New York: Pocket Books, 1972.

Morrison, T. *Playing in the Dark: Whiteness and the Literary Imagination*. Cambridge, Mass.: Harvard University Press, 1992.

Olsen, T. *Silences*. New York: Dell, 1983.

Ozick, C. *Metaphor to Memory*. New York: Knopf, 1989.

Sartre, J.-P. *Literature and Existentialism*. New York: Philosophical Library, 1949.

Sartre, J.-P. *Search for a Method*. New York: Alfred A. Knopf, 1963.

Schutz, A. *Collected Papers II: Studies in Social Theory*. The Hague: Martinus Nijhoff, 1964.

Shange, N. *For Colored Girls Who Have Considered Suicide When the Rainbow Is Enuf*. New York: Macmillan, 1977.

Taylor, C. *Sources of the Self*. Cambridge, Mass.: Harvard University Press, 1989.

Walcott, D. *Tomorrow, Tomorrow. The Arkansas Testament*. New York: Noonday Press, 1987.

West, C. "Black Culture and Postmodernism." In *Remaking History*, edited by B. Kruger and P. Mariani. Seattle: Bay Press, 1989.

Whitman, W. *Leaves of Grass*. New York: Aventine Press, 1931.

# Pluralism and the Tradition of Democracy

## JOEL KUPPERMAN

Among the many things to be avoided in talking about multi-culturalism, here are two. One is the temptation to give prizes to every group in all categories. It is generous and might seem likely to be good for the morale of recipient groups, but it can ignore reality. It is a simple fact, for example, that the world's greatest music has been written by Germans and Austrians who are now dead. All of these dead Germans and Austrians were men. There have been no great women composers of whom I am aware, though that can change and probably will.

We need to remind ourselves that the conditions that favor success in different categories are different. There are great novels written by women (from *The Tale of Genji* to *Mansfield Park* and beyond), even though women have produced no outstanding music and, before the late 19th century, no outstanding visual art. Similarly, the major achievements of African Americans in literature have not been paralleled in other arts. In the visual arts, there is no painter, sculptor, or architect of the stature of August Wilson or Ralph Ellison in literature.

My point is that areas of creative endeavor vary in their obstacles and opportunities, and so a group or culture can produce outstanding achievements in one area and less outstanding ones in others. This changes through time, as obstacles are removed, as opportunities open, and as traditions ripen.

A second thing to be avoided is the attempt to deal with a position or a tendency by pointing to something silly that exemplifies it. Positions on political and social issues rarely, if ever, are precise. They call for interpretation and also for extension or modification as new situations arise. Not all interpretations will be the same. And if an issue is of pressing general interest, not all interpreters will have anything like the same degree of intelligence, sensitivity, or common sense. This is especially true of the issues of multiculturalism and related matters of what has been called "political correctness."

In these areas, decisions often are made under pressure about what seem to be unprecedented problems and by people who are not well-trained in law or ethics. Some of these decisions are well-intentioned but very silly. My own university provides a prime example. At one point the student code sanctioned inappropriately directed laughter. A rule of this sort is virtually unenforceable, not only because of free speech (free laugh?) issues, but also because of the host of borderline and hard-to-formulate cases that it might seem to govern. The futility and absurdity of this rule should not disguise the fact that it was an attempt to make the campus seem less threatening to people who were ill at ease and easily upset.

One can use this failed rule as an example, but what I suggest is that it should serve as an example of people in the thankless role of education administrator scrambling to respond to what they perceive as changed circumstances, frequently without a clear idea of what they are doing. To condemn all attempts of this sort on the basis of some silly examples is to substitute cheap shots for argument. That something may be done badly in a given case is no reason for not doing it at all.

In the following paragraphs, I attempt to observe both of these cautions in talking about multiculturalism and democracy. I shall argue for the value of a serious educational multiculturalism — despite the examples that anyone can produce of silly forms of multiculturalism. I also shall argue for the unifying thread of a liberal democratic tradition, centering on tolerance and constitutional safeguards, for which one tradition, the Anglo-Dutch early American, deserves the prize.

The case for educational multiculturalism rests on two elements, neither of which should be ignored. One is the sheer quality of work, either non-Western or from disadvantaged groups in the West or by women, that would be left out of a narrow, traditional curriculum. The other is the benefit, both to white male students and to members of other groups, of a curriculum that takes a wider than traditional view.

That both of these factors matter has the following implication. The worth of a text should be a major factor, but not the only factor, in determining its inclusion in the curriculum. Not all non-Western or minority literature or literature by women is wonderful. There is as much that is weak, trivial, or shallow in these categories as there is in literature by Western males. Some of the sillier attempts at multiculturalism have involved putting some bit of Third World doggerel up against, say, Shakespeare. This is unfair, and it does not promote respect for Third World cultures among discerning students. It also is unnecessary, because great Third World literature does exist.

Let me mention some specific ways, from my own experience, in which non-Western texts — quite apart from the fact that they are non-Western — are especially useful. I teach undergraduate courses in ethics and social philosophy, both at the introductory and the junior-senior levels. Experience tells me that my students are happier and more focused if they are given a relatively small number of major works, rather than a large number of snippets, and if there is a high degree of contrast among the works they read, so that they are very aware of oppositions in viewpoint or perspective. One useful contrast in ethics is between philosophies that recommend a heightened and sharply focused involvement with some aspects of our lives, even if the challenges lead to suffering (for example, Nietzsche) and philosophies that recommend losing oneself in a way that leads to a tranquil, detached attitude toward one's life and society. Views of the latter sort are to be found in the West, but their greatest expressions are in the classics of Indian philosophy, such as the *Bhagavad Gita* or Buddha's sermons.

If one wishes to make the contrast triangular, a third element is a text that recommends neither a heightened and passionate involvement nor a detached withdrawal, but rather a moderate degree of involvement and concern with an emphasis on harmony and social responsibility. Plato and Aristotle are good authors for this position; but in my experience, Confucius or Mencius works at least as well. One reason to choose Confucius is the great importance that the texture of interpersonal relations assumes in the Confucian texts, along with a heavier emphasis on psychological observation. Both great Confucian philosophers repeatedly discuss tactics of self-management and how one can deal with one's own fallibility and learn from others. Aristotle has some important things to say about friendship; there is no sharp contrast in these matters between the classical Greek and classical Chinese texts. But overall, in my view, the balance tips in favor of the Chinese.

This connects with a contrast between much of Chinese philosophy and Western philosophy, especially Western philosophy of the last few hundred years. What might be termed *philosophy of life*, especially in relation to personal networks and the management of one's own nature, has loomed much larger in Chinese philosophy. This is something with which I had to come to terms in my recent book on character. It is not that no modern Western thinkers have had something of importance to say in this area of philosophy; it is rather that the best writers have not been seen as true philosophers (the Duc de la Rochefoucauld or Montaigne); they have been viewed as slightly bizarre (Nietzsche); or, as in the case of David Hume, the parts of the philosophy that deal with personal relations and the development of character get the least attention.

Therefore, much can be said, on the basis of its unique quality alone, for introducing a multicultural dimension into some instruction. Indeed there are benefits that are not a function of quality alone but also depend on other factors. In some ways the clearest and most impressive benefits are for intelligent white males. Some who promote multicultural education will want to

speak here of moral benefits, of increased sensitivity and tolerance. Of course, these benefits may be realized in some cases; but
one might be wary of emphasizing them for two reasons. One
reason is that they do not seem at all easy to demonstrate. The
other is that, if moral benefits are emphasized, there is a real risk
that multicultural education will take on the flavor of a pious
enterprise. Men and women of student age frequently do not like
being enlisted (or drafted) to serve in pious enterprises and likely will react accordingly.

A more predictable benefit of multicultural education is that it
will promote a greater sense of the variety of traditions, perspectives, and styles of expression. One comes to know more about
other cultures and subcultures. But one also comes to have more
perspective on one's own culture and subculture. The great
majority of students take the culture within which they are reared
for granted. However, one hesitates to identify that culture with
the tradition of Western culture for the simple reason that students' knowledge of Western culture typically is diluted and
sketchy, with a very minimal sense of the past. (Everyone who
teaches classic texts knows the difficulty that even bright students
often have nowadays in reading anything written before 1900.)
Nevertheless, the two terms of this unequal relationship have
some connection to each other. What students are brought up
with typically has something to do with the tradition of Western
culture. And usually they take their own culture for granted and
see it as uninteresting.

One's culture becomes interesting when one sees it as one possibility among many. It is possible, of course, that a student who
gets a sense of how other cultures are oriented may begin to see
her or his own as slightly crazy, just as students often begin to see
their parents as slightly crazy when they are exposed to different
styles of family life. These judgments can be affectionate. But
when they are harsh and condemnatory, often it is because an ide-
alization has been superseded by a partial acquaintance with
alternatives. Students who condemn Western culture as cruel and
exploitative in its dealings with other cultures typically have only

49

slight knowledge of how representatives of other cultures have behaved when they had power over others and were not subject to normal restraints. Given more knowledge, a student can see that the apparently singular wickedness of one culture is, instead, a problem rooted in human nature.

My suggestion is that multicultural education can give students more insight into their own culture, much as people who have traveled abroad come to notice more about their own countries. For white students, it reveals the peculiarity of the culture and may make Western culture more interesting. Students who identify strongly with other cultural traditions can begin to see that there are other possibilities — other non-Western traditions — so that the cultural map will no longer feature a simple polarity. Because multicultural study often involves different perspectives on familiar things, it also can play a major part in general intellectual development. This is because it is a major intellectual advance for a student to be able to hold two or more distinct ways of describing and classifying reality in her or his mind and to be able to see virtues and faults in each. Here I draw on an impressive study by William Perry Jr., *Forms of Intellectual and Ethical Development in the College Years: A Scheme,* published in 1970, which is based on interviews with undergraduates at Harvard University.

I view Perry's book as important partly because it connects with my belief that the most significant changes in a society often are nonpolitical and, because they are not decided as most political things are, can frequently slip through the awareness of most people. One example is the revolution in the late 1960s and early 1970s in attitudes toward sex and, more generally, gratification. It seems naive to attribute this change to sexual energies emanating from the Nixon White House. The greatest change in American education, especially higher education, in the last half century may be the increased (and more self-conscious) emphasis on exposing students to multiple perspectives on a single issue. Typically this change hits students when they come to college.

Perry explores the effects on his subjects of this disturbing and disorienting experience: At first the students are almost angry.

They want an instructor simply to give them The Truth, and the instructor typically refuses. At a more advanced stage, the students have cottoned on to what higher education is about. Everything is relative, they believe. There is no Truth, just a variety of viewpoints. At what Perry sees as the highest stage, this relativism has evolved into something else. A student now becomes aware that some perspectives have advantages over others and sees that there can be good reasons for allegiance to a particular perspective. Personal commitment is seen as compatible with awareness that there are always other perspectives available and that something can be said for them.

As much as I admire Perry's study, I see it as emblematic of its time — 1970 — and of the state of the best philosophical work at that time. On the other hand, in several relevant respects not that much has changed between 1970 and today. The one philosopher whose thought most prominently corresponds to Perry's scheme is Thomas Kuhn, whose *Structure of Scientific Revolutions*, first published in 1962, has had enormous influence in a number of fields outside of philosophy. Kuhn created a case, using historical examples, for regarding scientific knowledge as inevitably keyed to the perspectives, categories, and assumptions of particular scientific theories. There is, as the slogan has it, no neutral given: Any experience or observation is tinctured by the theoretical framework within which it occurs. This stance makes the comparison of competing scientific theories less straightforward than it traditionally had been.

Kuhn presses this point, dismissing any notion of a neutral, "objective" test. Because of this attack on the traditional assumption of scientific objectivity, some commentators have taken Kuhn to be a relativist, a label that he emphatically rejected. He has gone to some trouble to emphasize that his view does not preclude the idea of scientific progress, nor does he believe that the choice between competing theories is simply arbitrary (Kuhn 1970). His view corresponds closely to what Perry takes to be the highest level of thought.

Let us call Perry's and Kuhn's kind of philosophy, *perspectivism*. It might be thought that perspectivism is close enough to

51

relativism that it will undermine any sense that students might have that there are truths to be had and that there are positions that deserve one's personal commitment. But there is no simple answer to this, in part because of the variety of ways in which perspectivism can be held and communicated. Perhaps there are always both risks and gains in accepting perspectivism. The risks and gains both center on the way in which what had seemed forced on one by the nature of things now can seem a matter of personal decision and allegiance. The student can decide which perspective he or she prefers to adopt as the point of view he or she is at home in, so to speak. Thus one risk is greater self-centeredness, following the increased emphasis on the role of personal choice in systems of knowledge. Another is apathy, a sense that none of this really matters, that knowledge is just a game.

One possible gain is that reality can begin to look more interesting as one becomes aware of truths that become recognizable if viewed from one angle (although obscured if viewed from others). The gain that results from appreciating various points of view that, in the end, one rejects can also become significant, especially in areas such as politics. Perspectivism connects nicely with the emphasis of such thinkers as Michael Oakeshott on the element of conversation in politics. Perspectivism, in the final analysis, is a fact of the intellectual life of our time. One can no more ignore it than one can return to a medieval style of life. But, like most facts of intellectual life, it is kept from students until they enter college.

At any good college or university, students will be exposed to the way in which competing perspectives can be brought to bear on the same issue, such as intellectual or literary issues and (usually only in advanced courses) debates among scientists. But multicultural education should provide exposure to the way in which competing perspectives can be brought to bear on everyday life. For example, much Indian philosophy gives a view of the daily frustrations of goal-directed behavior that is very different from that, say, of Confucian philosophy. Confucians tend to regard the frustrations as inevitable, given a normal life of work within a community; though they emphasize that the frustrations will be less keenly felt if one keeps in mind one's major priorities, which should include at their center the controllable matter of being as good a person as one can be. Many Indian philosophers argue that this involves too much attachment to things and people that can slip away, and that a better strategy is to hold one's likes and dislikes at arm's length.

Literary works from more than one culture also can make students aware of different ways in which everyday life can be viewed. Three benefits accrue. One is that such study reinforces and extends exposure to competing perspectives on intellectual issues. Some of my students seem to regard much of their education as a kind of intellectual game that they are forced to play in order to gain the credentials that they want. They contrast it with real, everyday life, which they seem to think of as intellectually comfortable and unproblematic. If multiculturalism can make everyday life, too, seem problematic, then students may become less complacent and more ready to take seriously the problems of multiple perspectives.

Second, to be aware of conflicting perspectives in everyday life is to be more likely to take seriously everyday life as an object of reflective interest. Most people do not exercise much control over the development of their characters. David Hume thought that our greatest degree of control is typically through our choice of the circumstances and habits of life that, in turn, shape our characters. The "situationist" school of modern social psychology, in effect, endorses this view. Students, however, often have more time and ability to consider alternative versions of everyday life than they will have later on. Thus anything that promotes a reflective approach will likely help them to lead an examined, rather than an unexamined, life. Multicultural education can make a major contribution in this endeavor.

Finally, conflicting perspectives on, and versions of, everyday life carry with them the possibility of increased empathy for people who are different. One should not make too much of this. It is only a possibility, and furthermore there is no guarantee that increased empathy can produce sympathy: Skilled sadists seem to know exactly how their victims are feeling. Nevertheless, most people seem to function better with others if they have some degree of empathy for how others see the world and how they feel; and multicultural education can promote this empathy. I have seen this done intelligently in a secondary school by the assignment of such books as Richard Wright's autobiographical *Black Boy*, thus exposing teenagers to very different versions of everyday life. In this way, multicultural education can enable students "to appreciate and to evaluate ways of life other than those favored by their families," the importance of which for a democratic state has been pointed out by Amy Gutmann (1987), among others.

These are possible benefits of multicultural education for all students, and especially for white males. However, two caveats must be mentioned. One is that there are enough genuine accomplishments on the part of women, and on the part of every sizable minority group, that one does not need, so to speak, to paint the lily. Many pronouncements coming out of women's studies programs and various programs for minority studies are reminiscent of the Russian claims, in the late 1940s and early 1950s, to having invented such things as the telephone and the telegraph. My recollection is that this nationalist self-exaggeration stopped about the time of Sputnik. Of course, it had never been necessary.

There is a good deal of psychological evidence, going back to Matina Horner's "fear of success" studies in the 1960s, that many women and representatives of some minority groups have what amounts to a morale problem, which makes it more difficult for them to succeed. It seems plausible that being able to identify with highly successful women, or highly successful members of their groups, could alleviate this problem (Horner 1972; Bardwick 1971). To put it another way: A pattern of systematic discouragement can be countered by the encouragement of appropriate role models, which can be one of the functions of programs in women's studies, African-American studies, and so on. This encouragement seems to be consistent with standards of intellectual and aesthetic rigor. Large areas of American education have been corrupted by a "feel-good" mentality. There is nothing wrong with feeling good as a result of education, but education should not be unrealistic. Programs in women's studies and those oriented toward minority groups can achieve their purposes without being trivial.

My other caveat is this. It is simplistic to say that there should be a women's studies program or an African-American studies program without some specification of where such a program fits in a student's education. High schools distinguish between required courses and electives, and colleges often distinguish between "core" courses, on one hand, and advanced concentrations and elective courses on the other. The appropriateness of women's studies or African-American studies might depend on the required or "core" courses they follow. There is a great deal to be said for such programs *if* they are pursued by students who have an adequate grounding in what might be termed the traditional common culture of America. I will argue for the special value of political and social elements of that shared tradition in the final section of this paper. But for now, I simply will make the pragmatic observation that any country is in trouble if too great an emphasis is placed on centrifugal cultural elements, things shared by some groups and alien or antagonistic to others. The examples of Lebanon, Ireland, and the former Yugoslavia should remind us that pluralistic societies, despite the enormous benefits that I have been trying to suggest, also have their risks. A common educational base seems to be a good way of diminishing the dangers.

Earlier I mentioned my belief in the superiority of classical Chinese philosophy for the exploration of personal relations and everyday life. I now want to examine this topic in relation to controversies sparked by recent feminist ethics. This examination will lead to a description of the distinctive political and social merits of what I have termed the Anglo-Dutch early American tradition.

At the root of recent feminist ethics is the psychological research reported in Carol Gilligan's *In a Different Voice*, wherein the author claims that many (American) women see their ethical problems in terms of particular responsibilities growing out of their connections to particular people. This viewpoint would not give them a high rating in the scheme of moral development pioneered by Gilligan's late colleague, Lawrence Kohlberg. But the suggestion is that this scheme, which centers on an impersonal sense of impartial justice, is male-oriented. Furthermore, she suggests that there are advanced ways of thinking about ethical problems that are more characteristic of women and in relation to which Kohlberg's scheme is inadequate. Some subsequent, very interesting philosophical work links well with this suggestion. Christina Hoff Sommers, for example, has argued that the Kantian approach that subsumes obligation under general principles does not square with our sense of "differential pulls" in our obligations, so that we might have different and stronger obligations, say, to aged parents than to others. Interestingly, this notion suggests a subconscious Confucianism. Confucian ethics emphasizes the importance of special human connections, especially to parents.

My sympathy for the general tendency of this feminist ethics should be evident. Indeed we are talking not just about a philosophical debate but about what amounts to a cultural blind spot. An extreme example is the (probably apocryphal) story of the Victorian who, having been thanked for nursing a very sick spouse, murmurs that one was just doing one's duty. An ethics of duty and impersonal obligation misses a crucial part of life, an adequate sense of personal connectedness. Indeed, we typically criticize failures not as immoral but as lacking in humanity. A financier who cheats investors and a parent who entirely neglects a child are both open to criticism, but the traditional category of immorality seems more clearly appropriate to the former. The failure of the latter seems deeper somehow, and we wonder about him or her as a human being.

These views are essentially Confucian. One of the ironies of recent feminist ethics is its convergence on important points with the ethics of the extremely patriarchal society of ancient China. Indeed, one of the results I am hoping for, from continuing feminist scholarship, is a growing recognition among Western philosophers in general that everyday life and personal relationships not only are ethically important but also deserve to be the subjects of reflection. Everyone knows people who are highly intelligent and responsible in their public life, fulfilling their civic and professional duties, and yet are irresponsible and perhaps even mindless in their private lives. This, if I am right, springs from a cultural blind spot. It is not so easy to correlate everyday thought with philosophy, but it does look as if a weakness in ethical philosophy contributes to the blind spot.

Arguably, every culture has its blind spots. Traditional Confucian culture gets high marks for family values and for its intelligent attention to networks of personal relations. Students observed that classical Chinese poetry is more often friendship poetry than love poetry. But traditional Confucian culture gets low marks for its treatment of anyone who is disconnected from family or a personal support network. Derk Bodde, a distinguished sinologist who wrote an account of his Fulbright year in Peking, 1948-49, called *Peking Diary*, was struck by this. He commented, "Socially, the cohesion of the family is such that it gives a man strong claim on his relatives and immediate friends, but very little on the society as a whole"(Bodde 1967).

By contrast, ideals of impartial justice and an impersonal approach to issues of public ethics are distinctive merits of our national tradition. It is not, I hasten to say, that they are totally absent from other traditions; indeed, there is a strong hint of them when Confucius speaks of the one thread that connects his ethical observations and makes it sound like the golden rule (Confucius 1938). Rather, these ideals have an exceptionally clear and sophisticated development in our national tradition and in our ethics. Other traditions can learn from us, and we can learn from them. I have argued elsewhere that one ought to be able to construct a "bifocal" ethics, paying adequate attention both to the texture of private life and to the issues of public morality (Kupperman 1991).

In particular, I would concentrate on political and social thought in order to say a little more about the roots of the American tradition of democratic toleration. These roots include an ethics that emphasizes general principles and insists on impartiality. They also include the great literature of social contract theory, from Grotius and Hobbes through Locke and Rousseau. (In emphasizing the educational value of this thought, I am seconding Kermit Hall's point, in this volume, that it is important for teachers to learn more about the history of rights consciousness.)

One of the usual elements of social contract theory is the claim that human individuals are not hugely variable in their dangerousness, and that consequently every member of society must be considered in the design of society. The germ of an idea of equal, or approximately equal, rights for everyone is in this notion. The individual has these rights, furthermore, not because of family or connections, but because she or he is a member of society.

This in itself is distinctive, but there is more. The right to vote contains within it the possibility of being outvoted. In the early modern world, in which religious differences were a leading cause of violent mistreatment, a tradition began to develop in Holland (and more slowly in England) of tolerating people whose views might well seem offensive, stupid, or silly. Sir Thomas Browne's *Religio Medici* is a pioneering text in this regard.

Finally, there is at the root of our political and social tradition a skepticism about human nature that may go back to the doctrine of original sin or to careful reading of such classic texts as Plutarch's *Lives* (which was an especially popular book in America in the late 18th century). This idea is one of the reasons why we have a government "of laws rather than men" and the checks and balances so carefully written into the American Constitution. These ideas accentuate the impersonality of our political and social order. It has its unattractive side, by lessening the possibilities of public warmth and spontaneity. Someone who has an extremely sunny and optimistic view of human nature can see it as stultifying. But its value, which I believe is considerable, is in lessening the risks of long-standing abuses and in protecting us from social chaos.

This tradition is not drawn merely from a set of old texts and practices that have influenced more recent texts and practices.

There are habits of mind associated with it and resonances in popular culture. A frequent theme in the western movies of my youth was that one could not "take the law into one's own hands." More recently in popular culture there has been an increased emphasis on how valuable it is to be tolerant of people who seem at first to be "different." We tend to take many forms of tolerance for granted, and frequently it is immigrants who are most appreciative. My suggestion is that we can benefit most from a multiculturalism that incorporates these political and social attitudes at its base.

## Resources

Bardwick, Judith. *Psychology of Women*. New York: Harper & Row, 1971.

Bodde, Derk. *Peking Diary*. New York: Fawcett Premier, 1967.

Browne, Sir Thomas. *Religio Medici and Other Writings*. London, Everyman's Library, 1906.

Confucius. *Analects of Confucius*. Translated by Arthur Waley. New York: Vintage, 1938.

Gilligan, Carol. *In a Different Voice*. Cambridge, Mass.: Harvard University Press, 1982.

Glendon, Mary Anne. *Rights Talk: The Impoverishment of American Political Discourse*. New York: Free Press, 1991.

Gutmann, Amy. *Democratic Education*. Princeton, N.J.: Princeton University Press, 1987.

Horner, Matina. "The Motive to Avoid Success and Changing Aspirations of College Women." In *Readings on the Psychology of Women*, edited by J. Bardwick. New York: Harper & Row, 1972.

Kuhn, Thomas. *The Structure of Scientific Revolutions*. Chicago: University of Chicago Press, 1962.

Kuhn, Thomas. "Reflections on My Critics." In *Criticism and the Growth of Knowledge*, edited by Imre Lakatos and Alan Musgrave. Cambridge: Cambridge University Press, 1970.

Kupperman, Joel. "Tradition and Moral Progress." In *Culture and Modernity: East-West Perspectives*, edited by Eliot Deutsch. Honolulu: University Press of Hawaii, 1991.

Oakeshott, Michael. *Rationalism in Politics and Other Essays*. Indianapolis: Liberty Press, 1962.

Perry, William G., Jr. *Forms of Intellectual and Ethical Development in the College Years: A Scheme*. New York: Holt, Rinehart and Winston, 1970.

Sommers, Christina Hoff. "Filial Morality." *Journal of Philosophy* 83 (August 1986): 439-56.

# The Democratic Education of Disadvantaged Children

## BY BERNARD WATSON

When the founders of the United States were wrestling with the critical issues of their day, before and after the Revolution, they reiterated again and again that the youthful democracy could survive and flourish only if its people were well educated. Typical of the sentiments they expressed were John Adams' words in 1765: "Liberty cannot be preserved without a general knowledge among the people" — who, as his wife Abigail frequently reminded him, included women. Conscious of the tyrannical potential of both monarch and mob, these leaders believed that people could and should govern themselves. But, as Jefferson put it, "If a nation expects to be ignorant and free, it expects what never was and never will be."

In the intervening centuries, these statements have lost neither their significance nor their power, but — as the title of this book suggests — it is clear that as a nation we are still struggling with the question of how to educate our young people for responsible participation in a democracy. The task is exacerbated by the annual arrival of thousands of immigrants with little or no knowledge of American history and culture and often without any experience of life in a democracy. But it is complicated even more by the recent phenomenon of discrete groups — racial, ethnic, gender, disability, among others — vying for recognition and rights. The debates about identity, diversity, separatism, or multiculturalism are pursued with special vigor in our schools and colleges. The noise of these arguments makes it difficult to discern just what, if anything, is meant by "American" and sometimes drowns out the voices of those who are seeking a unifying common core.

In attempting to address the topic of education for democracy, I will begin with that quintessentially American icon, equality, and suggest that in education, as in other aspects of life, we are still far from realizing our ideal. I will then turn to social responsibility, a concept frequently honored more in the breech than in the observance, given the American penchant for "rugged individualism." Here, I will offer some examples of public policies that, through lack of foresight or by deliberate intent, have fostered inequality. Finally, I will suggest some characteristics of education that can ensure the future of our democracy by giving all our children the opportunity to learn and grow.

## Inequality

"We hold these truths to be self-evident, that all men are created equal, that they are endowed by their Creator with certain unalienable Rights, that among these are Life, Liberty, and the pursuit of Happiness." In these stirring words, the Declaration of Independence announced the fundamental principle of the American dream and set in motion the long struggle — continuing to this day — to clarify and interpret its meaning. The history of the United States is replete with landmarks of the effort to extend the promise implicit in those simple but profound words. The Civil War and the abolition of slavery, the guarantee of proportional representation, granting the vote to women, the protection of religious dissenters and suspected criminals, outlawing segregation based on race, including the handicapped and disabled as full participants in society — all these decisions and many others stand as monuments to the vision of the authors of the Declaration and the courageous perseverance of people who were not content with a limited definition and partial realization.

In our own time, equality of opportunity has been the rallying cry for those who see that gaining abstract legal rights, important as that might be, is not sufficient to overcome the constraints of the individual circumstances in which citizens were born and raised. What does it matter, they say, if you have the right to buy a house anywhere you want, but have no job? What use is your vote if you cannot read the ballot? What is the point of aspiring to be a scientist if your local school does not have a laboratory or offer calculus? In fact, why go to school at all if you are hungry, or are told you are a slow learner, or if you see that drug dealers are the ones with fancy cars?

How equal are the opportunities offered American children today? After years of good intentions and even actions, is the playing field yet level? Are all young people, regardless of family backgrounds or the communities in which they live, given the opportunity to live up to the expectation that they will become independent, healthy, and happy adults; responsible parents and employees; citizens who care about their country's welfare. For all too many, the *reality* is inequality. We have done a much better job with our senior citizens. The number of people aged 65 and older is growing, but all retirees receive Social Security and Medicare benefits, regardless of their need, and on average more than they contributed to the programs. Of the elderly, only 11% are poor. But 21.8% of our children — a total of 14,341,000 — live in poverty. Among African Americans, child poverty rises to 50%. (Poverty, by the way, was defined in 1993 as having an annual income under $14,350 for a family of four, or under $11,890 for a family of three.)

*The Reality of Inequality.* Contrast two babies. The first, a boy, is born to a teenage single mother who had no prenatal care and was addicted to drugs. *If* this child survives the neonatal intensive care made necessary by low birth weight and the complications of his mother's addiction, his problems are only beginning.

He may be neglected, abused, and not given even basic health care, including immunizations. He does not attend any kind of preschool. He lives in inadequate housing in a deteriorating neighborhood. He goes to a school where the teachers are largely inexperienced, bored, or hostile; they do not support or challenge him, and there are few interesting lessons and no class trips. Al-

63

most daily, he sees the drug traffic in full swing or experiences the violence of gang warfare. He considers dropping out of school, knowing that if he stays long enough to get a diploma, it will not be worth much. Even if he gets a job, which is unlikely, it will not pay enough to support a family.

Now imagine the other baby, a girl, born to an educated, well-to-do couple who are determined to give this child every advantage.

Her parents surround the child with emotional security, physical care, and intellectual encouragement. Although the public school system is considered to be among the best, she goes to an outstanding private school and receives special training in music, athletics, and ballet. Every year, she has opportunities to travel, to attend summer camp, or go to the beach. She gets into the college of her choice and begins the professional career for which she has been trained.

These scenarios may be extremes, but they represent the awful contrasts that are being lived out in this society today. It is certainly possible that the child of poverty may elude the fate of so many of his peers and overcome the obstacles placed in his way. It also is possible that the middle-class girl will *not* realize the hopes invested in her. The question, however, is why, in a society dedicated to equality, such unequal opportunities are tolerated and permitted to continue.

Here are some of the facts about the inequalities in American society. The statistics refer to African Americans, but members of other minority groups and white people at or near the poverty level do not fare well either.

*Income.* The median income of black males in 1990 was 60.8% of that of white males. The median income of black females was 80.7% of that of white females. It should be noted that these figures mask another continuing inequality: the median salary for white females is less than half that for white males (National Urban League 1992, p. 77).

*Wealth.* In 1988 the mean black net worth (bank accounts, stocks, home equity, and so on) was $26,130, or 23% of the mean white net worth of $111,950 (National Urban League 1992, p. 63).

*Unemployment.* The black rate of unemployment has been double or more than double that of whites for the past 20 years. Among black teenagers, as many as 50% are unemployed. And it must be remembered that only those still looking for work are counted; those who have given up the search altogether are not included (National Urban League 1992, p. 101).

*Housing.* Finding decent housing on a limited income is a problem for people of all races. In the past 20 years, family income has risen far more slowly than the cost of purchasing a home or renting one. In 1990, federal government "support" for home buyers through mortgage-interest tax deductions was $78 billion. In the same year, federal spending for public housing, rent subsidies, and other measures aimed at ensuring an adequate place to live was $18 billion (Children's Defense Fund 1992, p. 36).

*Education.* Education at all levels also is marked by inequalities. Consider, for example, the differences in the percentages of those who drop out of high school. The Department of Education, in its annual report, *The Condition of Education,* states that in 1990, 13.6% of all young people aged 19 to 20 had dropped out, 3.5% were still in school, and 82.8% had completed their high school education (rates that have remained virtually unchanged for two decades). However, within each group disparities appear: High school completion rates for whites were higher than rates for blacks, which in turn were considerably higher than rates for Hispanics (NCES 1992, p. 58). It should be noted that in many large urban school systems the dropout rate for minorities is considerably higher than that reported by the Department of Education, often approaching 50% or more. (However, when older groups are considered, the proportion that has completed high school is somewhat larger, reflecting the number of dropouts who later obtain GED certification.) Although minority high school completion rates over the past 20 years have improved, statistics such as these give little cause for supposing that equality in education has been achieved.

Another measure of educational attainment is the Scholastic Aptitude Test, the chief — although not the only — college entrance examination taken each year by about half of those who expect to graduate from high school. Minority participation has increased over the past two decades, but the verbal scores of all minority group students have continued to trail behind those of whites. (In the mathematics section, the highest average score was attained by Asian Americans.) The gap between white and African-American average scores has closed somewhat in both the verbal and mathematics sections, but it is still sufficiently pronounced to serve as a reminder of the inadequate preparation that many poor, black students receive in school (NCES 1992, pp. 223, 227). Studies have repeatedly shown a clear correlation between SAT scores and family income.

What about college? By their late twenties, most young people have completed their undergraduate education — or have given up any hope of doing so. The Department of Education, therefore, uses the population aged 25 to 29 years to assess educational attainment at both the high school and college levels. Here again, minority groups lag behind.

In l991, 55% of white 25- to 29-year-old high school graduates had completed one or more years of college, in contrast to 43% of blacks and 41% of Hispanics. In 1991, 30% of white 25- to 29-year-old high school graduates had completed 4 or more years of college, in contrast to 14% of blacks and 16% of Hispanics (NCES 1992, p. 62).

Statistics such as these indicate that severe disparities still exist in educational attainment, despite financial and other incentives for minorities (which often are criticized as unfair to students from the majority group). Common sense suggests that the explanation for the disproportionate distribution of college degrees is largely related to minority group poverty — inadequate elementary and secondary education, lack of encouragement and role models, and financial difficulties, among other characteristics. The disparities tend to reinforce themselves over time, thus creating what is often referred to as the "pipeline problem."

In this analogy, the education hierarchy is seen as an increasingly narrow conduit through which smaller and smaller numbers of students progress. For the few African Americans and other minorities who survive the "pipeline," the opportunities are many and varied as employers compete for their services. Unfortunately, when salary, inclination, and other considerations attract them into government or business, far too few individuals are available to take teaching positions, where they might serve as coaches and role models for minority young people.

An illustration of the way the pipeline problem works was given by Walter E. Massey, director of the National Science Foundation. In 1983, 9% of all college freshmen who planned to major in science or engineering were black. Six years later (at the point when the group that had started college in 1983 would presumably have completed their undergraduate work), only 5% of the bachelor's degree recipients in science and engineering were black. In 1990, some 13,600 Ph.D.s in science and engineering were awarded; only 2% (264) went to African Americans (Massey 1992, p. 1178). According to the Department of Education, less than half of the 1990 recipients of Ph.D.s of *all* races accepted faculty positions. For those with degrees in the physical sciences, 21%; engineering, 26%; life sciences, 47% (NCES 1992, p. 152). When these percentages are applied to the tiny number of African-American Ph.D. recipients — less than 300 — it is obvious that colleges and universities, and their minority students, have a serious problem.

The pipeline problem also affects the public schools. There is much evidence that students benefit from the presence of teachers of their own racial or ethnic group — individuals with whom they can identify, who understand their culture, who can inspire them to learn and achieve. Yet many school systems cannot, or at any rate do not, hire a sufficient number of minority teachers. In Los Angeles, for example, where racial and ethnic tensions are severe, the imbalance of Hispanic students and Hispanic teachers is especially pronounced. Here are the ratios as reported by the *New York Times* (16 February 1993). The student population of the Los Angeles public schools is 12.6% white; the teachers are 60.6% white. For African Americans, the percentages are 14.6% (students) and 17.2% (teachers); for "other" minorities, the percentages are 7.7% (students) and 9.1% (teachers). However, though Hispanics constitute 65.6% of the student body, only 13.1% of the teaching staff are Hispanic.

*The Results of Inequality.* It is clear from these examples that we have not realized the promise implicit in the Declaration of Independence. The persistent inequality of opportunity in American society, the social arrangements that permit some to live in luxury while others merely subsist on the margin with little hope of improvement, has many consequences. It would be foolish to suggest that all our problems would cease if, by the wave of a magic wand, we could immediately provide decent housing, adequate health care, and excellent education for all our citizens. Obviously, there are other factors that contribute to the dilemmas and dislocations we face: worldwide population shifts and political conflicts, the variety and rapidity of modern communication, or changes in the role of religion or the shape of the family.

Nevertheless, social inequality is closely bound with familiar situations and well-known problems that have been allowed to fester until they explode into newspaper headlines. Andrew Hacker, in his 1992 book, *Two Nations*, and more recently the Milton S. Eisenhower Foundation, conclude that 25 years after the warning of the National Advisory Commission on Civil Disorders, we still are divided into separate, unequal, and hostile groups and, therefore, still are threatened by racial and class warfare. The riots in Los Angeles may have been sparked by anger at the perceived injustice of a particular jury decision, but kindling for the fire had been accumulating over many years of neglect and the betrayal of hope. The conflagration was exacerbated by new ethnic hostilities unknown in the earlier Watts riots.

Conflict between newcomers and natives is a tragic and recurring theme in American history, and it is most severe in times of financial crisis and massive unemployment. When immigrants who have come in the hope of improving their lives are seen as unwelcome competitors for scarce jobs, racial and ethnic tension readily erupts into violence. Too often, those on the sidelines have indulged in what I call the game of "let's you and him fight," a convenient way of avoiding responsibility for rectifying the conditions that caused the strife. Little was heard — other than expressions of surprise — from the white establishment when tensions flared into violence between Hispanics and African Americans: in Los Angeles, over jobs in the Martin Luther King Jr. Hospital in Watts; in Washington, over construction contracts and government jobs.

Other negative consequences of unequal opportunity, most importantly in education, include the high cost — human as well as financial — of a welfare system that has trapped many women and children in a cycle of discouragement and dependency; an incarceration rate that, although higher in the United States than in almost every other country, has done little to diminish the fear of violent crime, particularly in our cities; and unemployment rates that, as noted earlier, are as high as 50% among African-American young people.

Meantime, the failure of the schools to prepare our youth for employment has become a prime concern of business and government leaders. One report after another has declared that 21st century jobs will demand high-level skills and technological expertise. Unless educational opportunity is increased, those newly entering the labor force (most of whom will be recent immigrants and members of minority groups) will be relegated to the shrinking market for routine service workers, while the nation is crippled by its inability to compete in the new global economy. It may be that the challenge of economic survival will accomplish the school reforms that have eluded other appeals.

## Social Responsibility

The rationale for espousing equality is multifaceted. Jefferson himself said that it was simply a "given," a truth of nature or of nature's god. Like his mentor, Locke, he believed that hereditary and other distinctions were merely artifacts designed to justify the pretensions of those who had accumulated power and wealth.

Others worry less about abstract religious or philosophical principles and simply take a pragmatic approach: Assuming that all have equal status before the law, and by extension equal rights to participation in the benefits of society, ensures that no individual will go unrewarded and that all will thus contribute to the welfare of the group.

From its beginning, the United States has thought of itself — and been regarded by other nations — as a grand experiment, an attempt to forge a new and better society based on equality. But the search for national identity has contained many contradictory images and impulses: a longing for stability, yet restlessness to explore the frontier; individual aspirations competing with the demands of the community; the serenity of life on the farm or in small towns juxtaposed against the excitement of the city. Initially and perhaps inevitably, given the circumstances under which the country was populated, the idea of "American" connoted "*not European*" — that is, not characterized by hereditary wealth and privilege, class distinctions, deference to king or pope, and numerous national languages and customs.

Americans, bound together by their common search for freedom from Old World persecution or restriction, and by the rapid ascendancy of English customs and language, could readily envision themselves as equals. (Slaves and Indians were entirely excluded from this picture of American-as-not-European.) Later, when consecutive waves of immigrants had to be absorbed, a new metaphor was needed and someone invented the concept of the "melting pot," in which cultural differences would be transformed into a uniquely American — and homogeneous — blend. The motto "e pluribus unum" took its place alongside equality as a defining principle of the New World.

Nevertheless, although there might be differences in emphasis or details, Americans have managed to forge a picture of what the United States *means* — or at any rate ought to be. The characteristics include a sense of national pride that encompasses both peace at home (the "domestic tranquillity" of the Constitution) and cordial relations with other countries; a democracy maintained by honest leaders and active, well-informed citizens; continuing progress in science, medicine, and technology, along with competitiveness in the world economy; cultural and intellectual creativity; mutual respect; and liberty and justice for all. It is a grand and glorious ideal; and though it has never been (perhaps never will be) perfectly realized, it has withstood attempts to dilute it, inspired reformers to reclaim it, and attracted both imitators and immigrants for 200 years.

*Why Inequality Persists.* With such a vision embedded in the national consciousness, why have such scandalous inequalities been permitted to occur and, even worse, to persist? There are many explanations, not least of which is the American ideology of rugged individualism, which sees each person as responsible for himself or herself alone and opposes government "interference" and higher taxes. Clearly, the racism that has afflicted this country since it was founded is a major contributing factor. Then, too, there is the typically American desire for short-term benefits, rather than long-range solutions, a preference that substitutes bandages for surgery for social problems. One also might cite our failure to recognize and deal with the consequences of change — demographic, economic, technological — perpetuated, in part, by the Norman Rockwell-like myth that small-town society is the "real" America. Certainly the great international crises of this century — the two world wars, Korea, the Cold War, Vietnam — have preoccupied national attention and diverted resources from domestic problems.

But what may be the most significant, and least understood, contributors to the perpetuation of inequality are deliberate government policies. The programs such policies established were good ones, forward-looking, designed with the best of intentions to adapt to changing conditions and to meet pressing national needs. In fact, however, they aggravated existing inequality, reinforced segregation, and fostered the urban crisis that threatens to undo us. Four such policies merit comment.

*Public Policy Concerning Transportation.* The move out from the urban core began in the 19th century with the establishment of cheap public transportation via electric trolley and commuter railroad lines. At first, new housing developments and even entirely new towns could be built only in areas to which these lines gave access. But after Henry Ford introduced his Model T in 1908, the scope for expansion was virtually unlimited. The American dream of a private home surrounded by greenery now was made possible by the apparently endless supply of undeveloped land and by the availability of low-cost automobiles. By the mid-1920s, Ford alone was producing 9,000 cars a day, or one every 10 seconds, and there was one passenger vehicle for every five inhabitants of the United States (Jackson 1985, p. 161).

Although privately owned, the automobile (and the truck) required new or improved public roads. That highways should be paid for with government funds was one of those critical decisions that had consequences undreamed of at the time. Not only vehicle owners, but practically *everyone* was in favor of street improvement: real estate developers and road builders; the entire array of those involved in the auto and oil industries; farmers, manufacturers, and retail merchants who saw that both cars and trucks could streamline the flow of goods and customers; and city fathers from New York to California who wanted to keep up with the times. Supported by federal, state, and local monies, streets were paved, widened, and extended into the countryside; restricted-access expressways soon became commonplace.

The policies begun in the 1920s were endorsed and expanded in the 1950s, when the "highway lobby" was successful in convincing Congress to pass the Interstate Highway Act (1956), which provided for 41,000 miles of roads, 90% of the cost of which would be paid by the federal government through the Highway Trust Fund, raised through non-divertible taxes on gasoline (Jackson 1985, p. 249). To date, gas taxes are a fraction of those levied by most industrial nations. Meantime, government support for mass transportation was negligible, and almost nothing was done to counteract the 30-year campaign by General Motors to eliminate streetcars and replace them with buses — manufactured by GM! As historian Kenneth Jackson notes, "unlike the road, which was defined as a public good and thus worthy of public support, mass transit was defined as a private business unworthy of aid. . . . Thus, Americans taxed and harassed public transportation, even while subsidizing the automobile like a pampered child" (Jackson 1985, p. 170).

A good highway system may well be deemed a necessity in a country the size of the United States, and so how can federal highway policy be considered anything but "neutral," conferring benefits on all citizens alike? Unfortunately, by not giving equal support to public transportation, this policy failed to take into account the needs of those who could not afford automobiles. Moreover, the new roads literally opened the way to the development of new suburbs and, aided and abetted by government *housing* policies, encouraged the flight of people and resources from the cities.

*Public Policy Regarding Middle-Income Housing.* Before the Depression, government involvement in housing was negligible. The economic collapse of 1929 was particularly catastrophic for homeowners (in the spring of 1933 there were more than a thousand foreclosures each day) and for homebuilders (between 1928 and 1933, residential construction fell by 95%) (Jackson 1985, p. 187).

Two New Deal measures are of particular relevance here. One was the Home Owners Loan Corporation, which established long-term, low-interest mortgages refinanced by the federal government. To protect the government's investment, HOLC also standardized methods of appraising housing value by developing a rating system for neighborhoods. Into its first (A, or green) category fell areas that were "new, homogeneous, and in demand." The fourth and last (D, or red) category was reserved for those that were "definitely declining" because of deterioration, vandalism, and the presence of low-income and minority families. HOLC did not invent the notion of equating an "undesirable" population with low real estate values and, in fact, made mortgage assistance im-

73

partial. But as a federal agency, it heavily influenced private banking decisions throughout the country and gave tacit governmental approval to the practice of "red lining" (Jackson 1985, pp. 196-203).

In 1934 another New Deal measure established the Federal Housing Administration to insure private loans for home construction and sale. Ten years later, a Veterans Administration program to assist returning military personnel to purchase homes was begun along similar lines, which included minimum construction standards, low down payments, and 25- or 30-year mortgages.

The negative effect, intended or not, of the FHA and VA housing programs was to increase the number of middle-class families escaping from the city. The programs promoted single-family homes, offered few funds for repair of existing structures, and favored areas of "relative economic stability" without "adverse influences." Entire sections of declining industrial cities were effectively condemned to further decay. When occasionally accused of discriminating against cities (or minority groups), the FHA was likely to reply that its mandate was stimulating home-building and buying, or reducing unemployment, *not* helping cities.

It should be noted that federal tax codes also have made their contribution to the promotion of suburbanization by allowing homeowners to deduct mortgage interest and property taxes from their taxable incomes. Renters have no such assistance. The billions of dollars that annually accrue to homeowners are seldom regarded as a federal subsidy, particularly when the topic is the high cost of welfare and other expenses related to the impoverished inner city.

*Public Policy Regarding Low-Income Housing.* Housing reform prior to the 1930s was largely a matter of establishing municipal codes to regulate sanitation, ventilation, and density. Early New Deal efforts to provide decent housing for low-income families were not successful, but the 1937 Wagner-Steagall Act empowered the U.S. Housing Authority to develop public housing projects by funding local agencies. Although eventually the projects provided for millions of people, the need always outpaced the available funds; and public housing was relegated to a low priority during and after World War II.

The most significant factor in increasing residential segregation was the requirement that an application for federal subsidies for housing construction be local and voluntary — a precedent established by a federal judge's ruling in 1935 that the Public Works Administration could not exercise the power of eminent domain to obtain land for its projects. As a result, towns and suburbs that did not want low-income people as residents were under no obligation to provide public housing; they simply did not create housing agencies and did not apply for funds. The preservation of the status quo was further strengthened by the legislative requirement that for each new unit of public housing built, a slum dwelling had to be eliminated. By definition, more affluent areas had no inadequate housing to be torn down (Jackson 1985, pp. 223-28).

As a result, most public housing was erected in poor and minority areas. When it was occasionally constructed in stable, middle-class neighborhoods, it provoked a mass exodus of the white population. The scarcity of land was at least partially responsible for the typical architecture of public housing: groups of high-rise apartment buildings that isolated tenants from one another, from street-level activity, and from community services and amenities. Symbolic is the Pruitt-Igoe development in St. Louis, which finally was torn down in 1976.

A last example of governmental contribution to the perpetuation of inequality is an area where government has failed to act.

*Public Policy Regarding Children and the Family.* "I have always been ready to learn," wrote former U.S. Surgeon General Dr. C. Everett Koop in 1992:

> But I am deeply concerned about the children who are not ready to learn. It's a national disgrace that at least 35% of our children, more than one in three, arrive for their first day of school lacking the basic good health that will enable them

to learn. Many are destined for school failure due to poverty, neglect, poor health and nutrition. Some 500,000 children are malnourished, while more than 12 million feel the pangs of hunger. Ten percent of American babies suffer from inadequate brain development caused by fetal malnutrition. Twenty percent of our preschool children have not been vaccinated against polio. (Koop 1993, in an NEA-sponsored advertisement)

Unlike most modern industrialized nations, the United States has no coherent family policy. Instead, there is a wildly uncoordinated list of programs that offer (usually inadequately) assistance with medical bills, supplementary nutrition for mothers and babies (the WIC program), or preschool education. Together, as author Sylvia Ann Hewlett says, they are neither cheap nor compassionate. She recounts the story of one young mother who could not afford private insurance but earned too much to qualify for public medical aid. Instead of the $1,000 worth of prenatal care that would have prevented the problem, her baby's hospital bills alone amounted to $150,000 — paid by the state.

> Our policies . . . tell the tale of a self-centered people supremely uninterested in the fate of other people's children — particularly if these children happen to be poor or black. . . . If you have a child, you are on your own. If you can look after it, fine. If you can't, don't expect Uncle Sam to bail you out. . . . The spirit of these tales is uncaring, even spiteful, and the thrust of the story is to deny any form of collective responsibility for children. . . . The public policies of. . . other nations demonstrate that babies are treasured and that childbirth is an event of enormous national significance. (Hewlett 1991, pp. 172, 176)

Hewlett evenhandedly places blames for the lack of a coherent family policy on both the conservative right and the liberal left. The former, she says, always have been reluctant to endorse a government role in matters affecting the family or children. They preferred the traditional (even if unrealistic) model of mothers at home and viewed state-run childcare centers and similar ventures as creations of "godless communism." Those on the political left, however, have been absorbed in promoting individual rights and have had little energy or inclination to consider the needs of the family — which many of them view as an institution that is outmoded, bourgeois, or worse.

Illustrative of the problem is the uncertainty surrounding President Clinton's announced goal of expanding Head Start to all eligible children. Dr. Edward Zigler, one of the program's founders, makes clear that Head Start often has been the victim of political maneuvering, since the day it was conceived as a way to use unspent War on Poverty funds allocated to the Community Action Program. For instance, the planning committee wanted to begin with a small, experimental summer program; but President Johnson's enthusiasm was so great that he insisted on starting up nationwide with more than a half-million children. He also made unrealistic claims for the program's benefits — increasing IQ, lowering the future costs associated with welfare and crime. Zigler comments: "I began to worry that the overselling, particularly the emphasis on IQ gains, would come back to haunt the program, and that too much was being promised too soon. As it turned out, my fears were, if anything, too mild" (1992, p. 27).

During this campaign, when Mr. Clinton called for huge increases in funding for Head Start, opponents were quick to challenge the alleged benefits of the program and to point to the poor quality of some Head Start centers. Some thought the program should be eliminated altogether. But as Zigler and others have pointed out, many of the questions now being raised are directly traceable to the fact that Head Start funding always has been precarious and insufficient. Research, evaluation, staff training, improved staff salaries — all of these would improve program quality, but they are apparently too costly.

Child advocates have bitterly observed that there is a simple explanation for the fact that 20% of American children (and up to 50% of African-American children) live in poverty, that there is no national policy in support of children and families, that Head Start currently serves only 36% of the children who are eligible. The explanation, they say, is that children do not vote.

By contrast, the elderly are very well organized. The American Association of Retired Persons is the largest membership group in the country. And they *do* vote. Politicians still shudder at the storm of protest provoked by the Medicare Catastrophic Coverage Act of 1988. It was repealed a year later after senior citizens by the million furiously opposed the idea that they be taxed to support better long-term care for the less affluent elderly.

The vast power wielded by the politically active elderly is a constant threat to any attempt to deal with the national deficit or to redirect resources. Hardly anyone, from the President down, dares even to hint at reducing the benefits paid out under the "entitlement" programs to the elderly (regardless of actual need) — Social Security, military pensions, government worker retirement plans — although these programs consume an impressive proportion of the federal budget.

Government policies certainly are not the sole constituent of "social responsibility," nor should they be. Community fabric is woven of many individual and local efforts; and, as de Tocqueville noted 150 years ago, Americans are unique in their desire and capacity to organize to aid themselves or others. Many take the obligations of citizenship very seriously, and many are generous in their contributions of money and time. In 1991 giving by individuals (including bequests) amounted to almost $111 billion (AAFRC 1991, p. 12), and a 1989 survey reported that more than half of all adults donated an average of four hours per week to volunteer work in hospitals, libraries, and numerous other non-profit agencies.

Both government and private efforts are necessary to maintain a good society, though sometimes, as I have discovered in my foundation experience, it is not easy to determine the proper role and boundaries for each. Conversely, the inequalities to which I alluded earlier also are the product of both government policies and private decisions, some merely thoughtless, others overtly racist. It seems to me that education is a most appropriate third element in this discussion, because providing equal educational opportunity is fundamental to overcoming other inequities and because that task is our most critical responsibility as a society. Unless good education is available to all, our democracy, our economy, and our culture cannot hope to flourish.

## Education

Americans have never been completely satisfied with their education system. Indeed, the great variety of our schools and colleges is a monument to the attempts by one group after another to make them more effective, relevant, or responsive to particular needs. However, the past decade has produced a remarkable flood of criticisms of American education along with numerous prescriptions for reform. Simply keeping track of them all is a full-time job.

Many of the recent reports have been motivated by concern for America's economy, particularly its ability to compete in the new global, information-based economy. One study after another, deploring the current or projected shortage of well-trained workers, has called for higher standards of education and improved achievement at every level. I am somewhat uncomfortable with this argument. Earlier "reforms" introduced at the urging of business and industry resulted in the very conditions now so often condemned: classrooms with fixed rows of desks, a piecemeal and lockstep curriculum, isolation and competition, bells and buzzers to signal the beginning and end of work, the teacher as "boss," an emphasis on order, quiet, and, above all, obedience. The "assembly line" model of education was implemented not only for the sake of efficiency but to prepare students for employment in the age of manufacturing. Industry may have moved beyond this concept, but unfortunately many schools have not.

Clearly, a major goal of education is to equip all students for satisfying and productive employment, but there are more important reasons for reforming education and resolving educational inequalities than ensuring the health of the economy. One is empowering each *individual* for a lifetime of exploration, independent inquiry, enjoyment, and reflection. Another — at the heart of

79

the earliest arguments for *public* education — is to ensure the well-being of the republic by inculcating respect for fellow citizens and a sense of responsibility for the common good. These aims must inform the discussion of education improvements and help determine the efficacy of specific proposals.

Perhaps we have had a sufficient number of studies and reports and conferences, particularly those that dwell on the pathology of public schools. We already know a great deal about what is needed, and there are many examples of schools that *do* succeed, often in spite of poverty, poor administration, and a host of other difficulties. I suggest that we need more coordination of existing information and more collaboration among agencies and professionals. Above all, we need the will to demand and implement reform.

Here are some benchmarks of a school or system that is on the way to serving the needs of individual students *and* the needs of American society.

*High Expectations.* At first glance this may seem obvious to the point of absurdity. But the fact is that many students are denied a quality education simply because they are written off almost as soon as they enter the school door. They are considered incapable of learning because they live in a poor neighborhood, or lack middle-class clothes and manners, or have difficulty with the English language. In some cases, this conclusion may be the result of unvarnished racism. Ironically, it also may stem from well-intentioned (though misguided and naive) concern: not wanting to expect "too much" of poor or black or Hispanic children, the desire to help them to "adjust" to the realities of their situation. For many years, such views have been given "scientific" undergirding by reliance on IQ and other test scores that purport to determine who is capable of learning and who is not.

The story of how testing began and then became so entrenched a part of American education is fascinating, but outside the limits of this essay. Suffice it to say that, while testing may be useful for diagnosing and curing academic deficiencies, it frequently has been misused. A low score on an early, single test can become like the mark of Cain, imprinted on the child's forehead and condemning him or her to permanent exile not only from association with "high-ability" students but from challenging teaching. From this insidious and widespread phenomenon spring such common practices as tracking, special education classes, and sorting students into college-bound or vocational education groups. Despite the many rationalizations for these practices, the damage to students' self-esteem and aspirations is almost incalculable.

Fortunately, some survive, in spite of their label. Not long ago, a friend described to me a high school reunion that brought together a number of distinguished alumni: an editor of a major newspaper, a Pulitzer Prize winner, the head of a health care agency, and others. As they shared their memories of their student experiences, they discovered a common thread: Not one of them had ever been advised to consider applying to college!

A commitment to quality education for all children must be based on the belief that all children can learn, that they respond to the expectations and standards of teachers and others in authority, and that all can be persuaded, pushed, or pulled into achievement. The experiments of Robert Rosenthal at Harvard some years ago plainly demonstrated the critical role played by teacher expectations. He picked some children at random and told their teachers that they were going to make unusual progress in the coming school year. And guess what? They did — apparently for no other reason than the teachers' high expectations. Numerous other teachers have reported that when students of varying abilities, backgrounds, and learning styles work together, it is by no means detrimental to fast learners and may well be the best way to inculcate mutual tolerance and true respect.

*Technology in the Classroom.* It is outrageous that today many, if not most, schools are not using electronic devices (particularly computers) as tools for learning — nor helping students to learn *about* these tools that will be an inevitable component of their working lives, whatever they choose to do. To deny today's students access to or familiarity with technology is as crippling as refusing to teach them to read. But unfortunately that is the case in many schools, particularly those located in poor, minority neighborhoods. Even schools that do have an ample supply of computers tend to use them only for routine practice assignments or for games, which is somewhat like limiting a Metropolitan Opera star to singing nursery rhymes.

Technology cannot and should not replace teachers; but it can be an immensely powerful asset in the educational process by permitting truly individualized learning, opening a wealth of information sources to budding researchers, and placing a class in touch with students halfway around the world. Whatever the obstacles to its widespread use — lack of teacher training, no money, bureaucratic intransigence — technology should be viewed as essential to the modern, quality classroom. Familiarity with technology is a requirement of almost any job that one can imagine, from retail clerking to medical science, from banking to manufacturing.

*Links Between School and the "Real" World.* "Relevance" may be an overused word, but true relevance is critical. In countless classrooms, in suburbs as well as inner cities, students are given a steady diet of monotonous lectures and dittoed worksheets. Understandably, they tune out; and boredom becomes one of the chief enemies of learning. But there also are numerous other places where young people are so excited about school projects that they go to school early and stay late — examining local ecology and planning environmental preserves, studying their ethnic heritage through interviews with senior citizens, or developing plans for a neighborhood teen center. They quickly recognize their need for more knowledge of English or math, history or science; and they absorb the necessary skills almost effortlessly. They also learn to work together to solve problems — a very different mode from the traditional pedagogy that emphasizes isolated work and competitive examinations. Unfortunately, the imaginative teachers and the freedom from routinized school schedules that are essential for this approach are not readily available.

The capacity to obtain a satisfying job with opportunities for new directions and growth is surely a necessity in a world marked by rapid economic and technological change. Yet many students, segregated by age and sequestered from the outside world, have little or no opportunity to find out what adults do for a living. Thus they have only the vaguest idea of how their skills and interests might relate to future employment. While college-bound young people will still have time to consider their future, this isolation is a major problem for the "forgotten half," as the Grant Commission termed the 50% of students whose formal education will end with a high school diploma.

A relevant education must include exposure to the world of work through meeting representatives of various jobs and professions, visits to offices and factories, and information about employment possibilities. Internships or apprenticeship programs that incorporate work and study have proved highly successful in Germany, but are available in this country only on an experimental and widely scattered basis.

Building on the experiences children actually have (ranging from TV to local neighborhood conditions) instead of an arbitrarily selected curriculum, using the school neighborhood as a site not only for learning but also for community service, allowing students to solve problems cooperatively instead of placing individuals in competition with all the others, encouraging older or more able students to tutor younger or less able children — these are some of the distinguishing features of effective education. Only when this kind of education becomes accessible to all American children can we begin to be satisfied that they are being properly prepared for a lifetime of democratic citizenship.

*Recognition of Changing Times.* Crucial to the reform of education is the reconceptualization of many practices, hallowed by time, that have not been closely examined. The "factory model" of schools already has been mentioned. Others are the length of the school year — which was designed to accommodate the need to have young people help out on the farm in the summer — and the length of the school day — which initially permitted students to get home in time to do chores, assuming that at least one parent would be there to supervise. Both the school year and the school day are too short for the needs of modern families.

Many schools still are ill-prepared to cope with their rapidly changing student populations, though in some places students may come from 20 or more different countries. Lack of understanding of or insensitivity to cultural differences can disrupt classes inside school buildings and spill over into neighborhood violence.

Yet another aspect of American education that needs radical overhaul is the cherished tradition of local control, which carries with it local financing of the schools. Although state contributions now equal or even surpass the local ones, there are great disparities in per-pupil expenditures within states. These expenditures range from $3,100 in Utah, Idaho, and Mississippi to more than $8,000 in New Jersey, New York, and Alaska (NCES 1992, p. 126). Many states have been wrestling with this problem. For example, at the time of this writing, the Texas legislature, caught between a court deadline and voter disapproval, was waiting to find out whether its latest plan for equalizing school funds (the fourth since 1989) will be accepted by a judge. In New Jersey, Governor Florio faced the threat of recall because of his efforts to provide more funds for education in such poverty-stricken cities as Camden and Newark.

*Equity.* Many of today's students need far more from their schools than the instructional program that once was considered adequate: nutrition, health care, supervised recreation and homework, loving support, relationships. The very definition of *school* needs to be expanded. This does not mean that teachers should take on additional responsibilities, but rather that school buildings should become delivery sites in which many types of services are offered by various professionals working collaboratively. As the African proverb says, "It takes a whole village to raise a child."

Schools must adapt to the student population they actually serve, not to the one they once had or wish they had still. Many educators believe or act as though they believe that schools can do as they used to do: offer a predetermined curriculum in an established way to eager respectful students. There are implicit assumptions about what children "should" bring to school, about the limits on what schools should offer children. Unfortunately, not all children come to school "equal."

Too many of the schools attended by the poor and minorities do not have even tolerable physical plants, equipment, and other learning resources — let alone "extra" services. The conditions in the Los Angeles system, as reported by the *New York Times* (16 February 1993), are depressingly typical, though California's problems are exacerbated by the sharp rise in the number of immigrants and the statewide recession. Children can learn under almost any conditions, but it is reprehensible to expect them to do so when they are cold or fearful, and in places that are dreary and dangerous. Random violence has forced many schools to resort to security guards and metal detectors. And no one seems to know what to do about the violence that lies in wait on the way to and from school or penetrates the supposed security of home.

Asking schools and other agencies to provide more services for some children, particularly those in low-income areas, may be viewed in a narrow sense as inequitable, undemocratic, or unfair. But to condemn any child to a less-than-adequate education (or to deny a child the minimum health and other care that makes learning possible) is not merely to fail them as individuals but to intensify the conflicts within our society, to hasten the decline of America's hard-won — and enviable — position, and to renege on the promise of America. At present, the United States is the only advanced society in which the young are worse off than the elderly. If children are America's prime resource, as surely they are, then the inequities in our treatment of them must be resolved. What is good for them is good for us all.

## Unity

Should education for democracy take a form with disadvantaged children that is different from what is right for middle-class children? Absolutely not!

There are two kinds of fundamental change that I view as essential. The first is equalizing the opportunities available to poor and minority children, which means bringing their school buildings and the services available to them up to the standard enjoyed in middle-class communities. That change is fairly straightforward, will cost a considerable amount of money because of the years of "deferred maintenance," and is long overdue. The second is somewhat more complex: providing an effective education to *all* students in *all* schools. I have tried to identify some of the educational attitudes and practices that I believe are necessary to ensure our political, economic, and cultural health.

I had hoped that the very idea of separate education for certain groups had long since been discredited, because in the past it so often turned out to be unequal. Unfortunately, there are a number of African Americans and others who have been advocating a new form of segregation for black children on the grounds that these children will develop both skills and self-esteem only when taught by teachers of color using an Afrocentric curriculum. While I understand the frustration and anger that have motivated this development, I am opposed to it on numerous grounds. One is my certainty that African-American children will be ill-prepared for life in 21st century America after years spent in the confines of a narrow curriculum. Whatever education for democracy may mean, it surely must include exposure to difference, variety, new ways of thinking, other people's myths and histories, dances and artifacts, humor and religion.

Robert Hughes, the internationally renowned historian and art critic, reflecting on his "monocultural" schooling in the Australia of the 1950s, recalled that it was intended to "prepare us to be little Englishmen and Englishwomen, though with nasal accents." He commented:

The history of Spaniards in America is not for Hispanics alone. The history of blacks is not for blacks alone. No minority or group can be written out of American history, because the very nature of its narrative enfolds them all. This polyphony of voices, this constant eddying of claims to identity, is one of the things that makes America America. (Hughes 1993, p. 95)

There never was a core America in which everyone looked the same, spoke the same language, worshipped the same gods and believed the same things. Even before the Europeans arrived, American Indians were constantly at one another's throats. American is a construction of mind, not of race or inherited class or ancestral territory. (Hughes 1993, p. 12)

Finding the proper relationship between this country's diversity and the idealistic dreams that have been central in its history — particularly equality for all its citizens — is as great a challenge as we have ever faced. Recently, some commentators have suggested that the racial and ethnic conflict in the United States is part of a worldwide phenomenon and may escalate to the levels of violence now found in Eastern Europe, Sri Lanka, India, and elsewhere. One recommendation being heard more frequently is immigration restriction, as is being proposed in some countries (Germany and Great Britain, for instance). But that would do little to resolve the intergroup tensions we already are confronting.

It is my profound hope that the American experience will continue to be unique. I hope that we will find the resolution to struggle — together — toward the realization of a society that offers all its children the opportunity to succeed, seeing our differences as strengths and our unity in loyalty to the American experiment in democracy. It is in the public schools of this nation, the "common" schools, reformed to be truly equal and excellent for all, that we have the best and perhaps only chance of achieving that goal.

## References

AAFRC Trust for Philanthropy. *Giving USA 1992: The Annual Report on Philanthropy for the Year 1991.* New York, 1991.

Children's Defense Fund. *The State of America's Children, 1992.* Washington, D.C., 1992.

Hacker, Andrew. *Two Nations: Black and White, Separate, Hostile, Unequal.* New York: Charles Scribner's Sons, 1992.

Hewlett, Sylvia Ann. *When the Bough Breaks: The Cost of Neglecting Our Children.* New York: Basic Books, 1991.

Hughes, Robert. *Culture of Complaint: The Fraying of America.* New York: Oxford University Press, 1993.

Jackson, Kenneth T. *Crabgrass Frontier: The Suburbanization of the United States.* New York: Oxford University Press, 1985.

Koop, C. Everett, M.D. "American Achievers." Special advertising feature sponsored by the National Education Association in *Time* (Top Management Edition), 1 February 1993.

Massey, Walter E. "A Success Story Amid Decades of Disappointment." *Science,* 13 November 1992, pp. 1177-79.

The Milton S. Eisenhower Foundation. *Investing in Children and Youth, Reconstructing Our Cities.* Washington, D.C., 1993.

National Center for Education Statistics (NCES). *The Condition of Education, 1992.* Washington, D.C.: U.S. Department of Education, 1992.

National Urban League. *The State of Black America, 1992.* New York, 1992.

Wood, George H. *Schools that Work: America's Most Innovative Public Education Programs.* New York: Dutton, 1992.

Zigler, Edward, and Muenchow, Susan. *Head Start: The Inside Story of America's Most Successful Educational Experiment.* New York: Basic Books, 1992.

# PART II

# Constitutional Imperatives

# Constitutionalism in Education for Democracy

## BY JOHN J. PATRICK

In 1776 Americans were deeply involved with the problem of constitutionalism, of how to create a government with sufficient power to provide necessary public services and with sufficient limitations to prevent tyranny.[1] They sought the elusive condition of ordered liberty to secure the rights of individuals in civil society. Their attempts to combine power and restraint, order and liberty, in one coherent system produced profound arguments on the meanings and operations of constitutional government. These arguments of the American founding era are relevant to the concerns and challenges of democratic citizenship today. Therefore, the ideas on different sides of these founding-era debates should be in the core curriculum of any school with the goal of educating students to become responsible citizens of a constitutional democracy.

How should the founding-era constitutional debates be included in the school curriculum and used in the classroom? My response to this question involves three topics: 1) purposes and first principles of constitutional government in the arguments of American founders and the civic education of students today, 2) key documents for civic education that exemplify the founding-era consensus and controversy about constitutionalism, and 3) imperatives of teaching and learning about American constitutionalism and democratic citizenship.

## Purposes and First Principles

An ostensible concern of constitution makers is how to effectively grant and limit the powers of their government (Sunstein

1988). But the ultimate questions, the most important concerns, are normative. They pertain to the ends that will be served by grants and limitations of power (Diamond 1981, p. 129). In 1776 John Adams of Massachusetts stressed the critical importance of clarity and care in deciding both the ends and means of a proposed constitution. In his incisive essay, *Thoughts on Government*, written at the outset of the grandest burst of concentrated constitution making the world has ever seen, Adams wrote:

> [T]he blessings of society depend entirely on the constitutions of government. There can be no employment more agreeable. . . than a research after the best. [Alexander] Pope flattered tyrants too much when he said,
>
> > "For forms of government let fools contest,
> > That which is best administered is best."
>
> Nothing can be more fallacious than this. . . . Nothing is more certain from the history of nations, and the nature of man, than that some forms of government are better fitted for being well administered than others. We ought to consider, what is the end of government, before we determine which is the best form. (Schechter 1990, p. 129)

Key questions, then, of constitutionalism and constitution makers are always about the proper purposes of government. These questions about governmental power, its latitude and limits, ought to be at the center of civic education for constitutional democracy. And they ought to yield defensible criteria by which students and citizens make judgments of good or bad — better or worse — about the structure, operations, decisions, and legitimacy of their constitutional government; and by which they compare, contrast, and evaluate different polities of different times and places.

There was a remarkable agreement on purposes and first principles among different parties of the American founding-era debates on constitutional government. John Adams, for example, tapped an emerging American consensus to emphasize the following purposes and first principles of constitutionalism in *Thoughts on Government*:

- Good constitutional government is "an empire of laws" in which the rule of law prevails over the arbitrary will of men.
- Good constitutional government is republican, based on the consent and sovereignty of the people and authentically representative of the will of the community.
- Good constitutional government secures the inalienable rights of individuals against tyranny from any source, whether it be the tyranny of one, a few, or many.
- Good constitutional government permits the greatest happiness for the greatest number of people by establishing conditions of liberty and order that maximize opportunities for individuals to satisfactorily pursue personal fulfillment in civil society.

Adams' purposes and first principles were compatible with core ideas of *The Federalist Papers*, written in 1787-1788 to defend the U.S. Constitution during the arguments on ratification. They also were agreeable with the writings of leading Anti-Federalists, using pseudonyms such as Brutus, Cato, Federal Farmer, and Centinel, who opposed the Constitution of 1787. Co-authors of *The Federalist Papers*, James Madison, Alexander Hamilton, and John Jay endorsed these core civic ideas. And so did Melancton Smith, Richard Henry Lee, Patrick Henry, and George Clinton, who ably represented the Anti-Federalist opposition (Bailyn 1992; Lutz 1988; Richards 1989; Sinopoli 1992).[2] Even Adams' nemesis, Thomas Paine, who argued acidly with Adams about institutions and operations of government, tended to agree with his political foe on the most fundamental purposes and principles of good constitutional government.[3]

A fundamental lesson of American civic education is that the arguments of the founding era were conflicts within a broad consensus on the desirability of constitutional republicanism (what we today refer to as representative constitutional democracy). Contending groups, such as the Federalists and Anti-Federalists, generally agreed on the ends of constitutional government, such as simultaneous security for the public good and the private rights of individuals. Both Publius (the Federalist) and Brutus (the Anti-Federalist) fundamentally valued representative government, the rule of law, popular sovereignty, civic virtue, public good, and individual rights.[4] The sharp disagreements then, as today, were about the exact meanings and practical applications of these core ideas in the operations of constitutional government and the lives of citizens.

The conceptual agreements and operational disagreements of the founding-era political thinkers can be synthesized for pedagogical purposes around three central, continuous, and interconnected paradoxes of constitutional republicanism (representative democracy): 1) how to achieve liberty and order, 2) how to have majority rule and minority rights, and 3) how to secure the public good and the private rights of individuals. These were the key problems for all sides to the American founding debates on the meaning and practice of constitutionalism in a republic, and they are central challenges today for those who would sustain and improve upon their civic inheritance from the founders. These three intertwined paradoxes, therefore, should be pervasive parameters of inquiry for students who would know the complex challenges of making and maintaining a constitutional and democratic political order committed to the achievement of liberty for its citizens.

Each of these paradoxical relationships involves questions about constitutional limits. For example, at what point and under what conditions should the power of the democratic majority in government be limited by the higher law of the Constitution to secure the rights of individuals in the minority? And at what point and under what conditions should the liberty of individuals be limited by law to protect and sustain the democratic authority of majority rule? Alternative responses to these basic questions have raised critical constitutional issues throughout the history of the United States, from the founding era until the present. Numerous landmark decisions of the U.S. Supreme Court have dealt with these questions, as have controversies between the major political parties during national elections and sessions of Congress.

From the 1780s until today, Americans have debated about 1) when and how to limit the power of the people's government to protect the inherent rights and liberties of each person, and 2) when and how to limit individual rights to liberty or privacy for the public good, as determined by representatives of the majority of the people. These questions are as vital today as they were more than 200 years ago.[5]

A rich legacy of literature is available for students of the founding-era arguments on the paradoxical questions about the meaning and practice of constitutional republicanism (representative democracy). These primary documents should be the raw materials of civics lessons on the core concepts and continuing controversies of democratic constitutionalism. The pedagogical problem is to select a few of the very best documents, from the vast number available to us, and to organize them effectively for teaching and learning in the classroom.

## Key Documents

The Declaration of Independence, the first founding document of the United States, can be a point of entry for in-depth study of the founding-era arguments on constitutionalism because it proclaims succinctly the American consensus on the purposes of government: security for the "unalienable rights" of individuals and government by "consent of the governed." The constitutional values of majority rule with minority rights, public good with private rights of individuals, and ordered liberty are connoted throughout this document.

The Declaration of Independence calls for limitations on any kind of power, including the democratic power of the people, in order to secure the "unalienable rights" of every person. A good constitution is one that secures these rights. Thus key ideas of the Declaration of Independence are foundations of American constitutionalism, and they can be used as criteria by which one judges the worth of a constitutional government (Anastaplo 1989, pp. 1-29; Berns 1992, pp. 11-20). According to Walter Berns,

"We were first constituted by the Declaration of Independence, and the Declaration must figure prominently in a proper study of American constitutionalism" (p. 19).[6]

The "Declaration" presents examples and reasons about the failure of British government to fulfill the purposes of good government. By implication, the American constitution-makers were challenged with the mission of succeeding, where the British had failed, in establishing good governments for the United States of America in terms of widely accepted criteria stated in the Declaration of Independence. The primary criterion, of course, is this one: "That to secure these Rights [to life, liberty and the pursuit of happiness] Governments are instituted among Men, deriving their just Powers from the Consent of the Governed." All persons, of course, are equal in their possession of certain "unalienable rights."

American constitution-making already was under way in several states by the time the Declaration of Independence was written. And the constitution makers worked from long and strong traditions of republican government that had developed during more than 150 years of the American colonial experience (Lutz 1988, pp. 35-69). Several of the original state constitutions, and the processes of making them, are worthy of consideration for civic education purposes. Two of them, however, are especially clear and useful exemplars of the consensus on principles and controversy about practices that marked the founding-era debates. These two frames of government recommended for comparative analysis and evaluation by civics students are 1) the Pennsylvania Constitution of 1776 and 2) the Massachusetts Constitution of 1780.[7]

The Pennsylvania document exemplified, to a considerable extent, institutional arrangements and civic values compatible with Anti-Federalist constitutionalism as it was expressed in 1787-1788. By contrast, the Massachusetts Constitution, drafted primarily by John Adams, was a forerunner of Federalist constitutionalism. The Pennsylvania document's unicameral legislature, virtual legislative supremacy, judicial accountability to the legislature, and provisions for limited terms, frequent elections, and rotation in office, for example, were later used by Anti-Federalist writers, such as Brutus and Centinel, in their arguments about the characteristics of good government. The Massachusetts document's separation of powers, bicameral legislature, executive veto, and independent judiciary were precursors of the federal Constitution of 1787, the model of Federalist constitutionalism, and the target of Anti-Federalist constitutional criticism.

The discourse and debates of the Anti-Federalists and Federalists are a profound extension of the founding-era arguments about the principles and practices of constitutional governments in the original thirteen states. Brutus, the Anti-Federalist, was as adamant as Publius, the Federalist, about establishing constitutional government that would "secure the liberty of the citizens of America" and "admit a full and fair representation of the people" (Storing 1981*b*, p. 113). But Brutus, unlike Publius, tried to demonstrate "that the powers [in the Constitution of 1787] are not properly deposited for the security of public liberty" (Storing 1981*b*, p. 123). Brutus, for example, emphasized broad majority rule and citizen participation in a representative constitutional government that directly reflected the popular will. Publius wanted a government based on the popular majority, but limited effectively by the higher law of the Constitution to protect rights and liberties of individuals in the minority. Publius, more than Brutus, wanted to constitutionalize, or limit, the democratic will of the people, because he feared, more than Brutus did, majoritarian tyranny.[8]

Serious study of Federalist and Anti-Federalist ideas is a key to understanding the civic culture of the United States and the perennial and paradoxical problems of constitutional democracy: how to simultaneously and reasonably achieve liberty with order, majority rule with minority rights, and the public good in concert with the private rights of individuals. The best *Federalist Papers* on these core dilemmas are numbers 1, 9-10, 14-15, 23, 37, 47-51, 70, 78-81, and 84. The best Anti-Federalist counterpoints are found in several essays by Brutus (numbers I-V and X-XV) and Federal Farmer (I-VII and XVI-XVII).[9]

Careful comparative analysis of *Federalist* 10 and 14 and *Brutus* I and IV will yield a deep understanding of their contrasting conceptions of republicanism and liberty, which explain their differing views on representation in government, majority rule, security for individual rights, popular sovereignty, social pluralism, and the public good. Comparative analysis of *Federalist* 78 and *Brutus* XV will frame a continuing constitutional controversy about the make-up and functions of the judiciary in a democratic political order.

Brutus, for example, argued that the independent federal judiciary of the 1787 Constitution was antithetical to the very idea of a free, popular, majoritarian government.[10] He said, "I question whether the world ever saw, in any period of it, a court of justice invested with such immense powers, and yet placed in a situation so little responsible [to the people]" (Storing 1981, pp. 182-87). By contrast, Alexander Hamilton, as Publius, expressed a rebuttal in *Federalist* 78. He argued for an independent judiciary, exercising judicial review, as an indispensable instrument of constitutionalism with the ultimate purpose of securing individual rights against all potential sources of tyranny, including democratically elected legislative assemblies (Cooke 1961, pp. 521-30).

The contending ideas of Federalists and Anti-Federalists on perennial problems of democracy have been connected to alternative visions of constitutional democracy throughout U.S. history, from the founding era to the present (Peterson 1992). Arguments about the role, powers, and constitutional makeup of the federal judiciary, which are reminiscent of the Publius-Brutus debate, have persisted until today. Thomas Jefferson, for example, lambasted the John Marshall Court in terms and tones compatible with the position of Brutus. Chief Justice Marshall, of course, directly drew on the writings of Hamilton, as Publius, to justify his use of judicial power to serve the highest purposes of American constitutionalism. Any avid reader of 20th century newspapers knows that the terms and spirit of the founding-era debate on the federal judiciary have been replicated, with only slight modifications, in our own times (Peterson 1992, pp. 121-26).

There were prominent Anti-Federalist ideas in the Populist and Progressive crusades to reform democratic government from the 1890s until the 1920s. Today's "term limits" constitutional reformers are acting on an old Anti-Federalist idea (Peterson 1992, p. 114). And the "term limits" opponents usually justify their views with arguments that Publius, the Federalist, would have approved. Furthermore, the central themes of Brutus and several other Anti-Federalist writers are compatible with the views of our contemporary advocates of communitarianism and "strong democracy" based on deep civic commitments and extensive citizen participation for the public good (Barber 1984 and 1992; Bellah et al. 1991). By contrast, Publius in *The Federalist Papers* is the founding-era precursor of our current proponents of "liberal purposes" and "liberal virtues" in constitutional democracy (Galston 1991; Macedo 1990).[11]

The great founding-era scholar, Herbert Storing, emphatically and eloquently stated the importance of the Federalist versus Anti-Federalist debate for civic education and citizenship today. Storing said, "If . . . the foundation of the American polity was laid by the Federalists, the Anti-Federalist reservations echo through American history; and it is in the dialogue, not merely in the Federalist victory, that the country's principles are to be discovered" (1981, p. 72).

## Imperatives of Teaching and Learning

The ideas and issues of the founding-era dialogue and debate on constitutionalism are forever relevant to people committed to the complex conjoining of liberty and order, majority rule and minority rights, and public good and private rights of individuals. Systematic teaching of these ideas and issues on constitutionalism, therefore, is a first imperative of civic education for democracy.

The core ideas on constitutionalism have framed more than 200 years of political debate in the United States, and they have become interesting to people around the world, now more than ever, as we enter what historians of the future may call a "New

Global Age of the Democratic Revolution," after R.R. Palmer's great study of the 18th century "Age of the Democratic Revolution" (1959).[12] However, students in our schools, the future participants of our political order, will neither know nor value these core civic ideas unless they have regular opportunities to learn the constitutional thought of the American founders, Federalists and Anti-Federalists. Furthermore, if young people in school are not substantially exposed to documents that contain the constitutional ideas of the founders, they cannot be expected to think critically about these ideas in order to identify and maintain the best of them, and to modify and improve upon the rest of them (Butts 1989).

A key to better teaching and learning of founding-era conceptions of constitutionalism and their subsequent development in American and world history is emphatic, detailed, and recurrent treatments of these ideas in the classroom. The core ideas and issues must be introduced early in the curriculum and visited again and again, in cycles of increasing complexity and depth, if students are to develop a deep understanding of the ideas and reasoned commitments to them as first principles of constitutional democracy. A recent summary of findings from twenty years of the National Assessment of Educational Progress (NAEP) concluded that "students who reported 'a lot' of study of U.S. history and civics topics [including the Constitution and constitutional issues] also had a higher proficiency in those subjects" (Mullis et al. 1990, p. 71).

A second imperative of constitutionalism in education for democracy is intellectually active learning by inquiring students, such as the 1) interpretation, criticism, and discussion of primary texts on constitutional thought; 2) analysis and debate of constitutional issues; and 3) participation in classroom simulations (for example, a simulated ratification debate of the founding era or a mock congressional hearing on a proposed constitutional amendment of our own times).[13] Active learning by inquiring students appears to be associated with greater achievement of knowledge and development of cognitive capacity for problem solving and critical thinking, which are requisites of responsible democratic citizenship. In the latest NAEP study on civics, students who reported regular or extensive participation as active learners in the classroom "tended to perform better in the assessment than their peers who had occasionally or never participated in these activities" (NAEP 1990, pp. 83-85).

A third imperative is ongoing inquiry and critical thinking about ideas and issues in an open classroom climate, which leads to higher levels of achievement and development of positive orientations to democratic attitudes. In an open classroom climate, students feel free and secure about expressing and examining ideas and issues, even those that are unconventional or unpopular. In an open classroom climate, the teacher is emphatically supportive of freedom of expression and inquiry about controversial topics. Furthermore, the teacher serves as a model and mentor for students in their collegial pursuit and use of knowledge to formulate, examine, and justify positions on constitutional issues (Leming 1985, pp. 162-63).

Systematic and intellectually active learning about ideas and issues of constitutionalism, in an open classroom climate, appears to be the way for students to develop profound knowledge and support of core principles of constitutional democracy, which are the essential elements of an American civic creed.[14] To be an American has been, in large part, to acquire, to believe in, and to act on these core civic ideas. Thus a fourth imperative of teaching and learning about constitutionalism is developing commitments among students, based on reason, to these core civic ideas.

An American identity based on common principles of constitutional government was an invention of the founding era. The historian Edmund Morgan (1977, p. 100) reminds us that, "Nationalism has been the great begetter of revolutions. . . . In our case it was the other way round. We [Americans] struck for independence and were thereby stirred into nationality; our nation was the child, not the father, of our revolution."

James Madison and other American founders nurtured this "child" — American national identity — with novel notions of constitutionalism based on "a popular sovereignty not hitherto fully recognized," says Edmund Morgan. "Madison was inventing a sovereign American people [in an extended national republic] to overcome the sovereign states" and unbridled diversity, which threatened political union, the public good, and the private rights of individuals (Morgan 1988, p. 267).

Political philosopher David Richards concurs with historian Morgan's views about the centrality of new civic principles in the creation of a new American community of the founding era. Richards (1989, p. 295) notes that the founders' "new conception of political community (a community of principle) was. . . argued over and justified to the people at large in terms of . . . the ends of politically legitimate government (respect for rights and pursuit of the public good)." This "community of principle" alone gives long-term hope for maintenance of national community and unity in the increasingly diverse American society. It is the cohesive civic core of a multicultural country, which Americans of various classes, religions, regions, races, and ethnic origins have in common. This "community of principle" also is the foundation for fruitful continuing critical inquiry and judgments about the nature and uses of constitutional democracy in the United States.

In 1787 James Madison everlastingly framed the central issue for inquiry and political action in America's pluralistic constitutional democracy. In *Federalist* 10 he wrote, "To secure the public good and private rights against the danger of [an overbearing majority], and at the same time to preserve the spirit and form of popular government is then the great object to which our inquiries are directed" (Cooke 1961, p. 61). Thus Madison recognized both personal liberty (private rights) and community concerns (public good) as potentially compatible goals of constitutional government in the United States (Ketchum 1993, p. 172). And so it is today. Our inquiries and actions as civic educators, students, and citizens still must be centrally concerned with conjoining the sometimes, but not necessarily, contradictory factors of public and private goods, of community and individuality, of majority will and minority rights, and of unity and diversity. This kind of inquiry requires that we reject the rigid polarity of either/or thinking and favor the flexible "more or less" way of thinking, to balance and blend opposing forces that must be successfully joined to sustain a free society.

In our pursuit of this never-ending inquiry on constitutionalism, we might tend to emphasize individualism, pluralism, and private rights more than majoritarianism and public community, as some Americans have done since the founding era. Or we might lean more toward the side of community, unity, and public duty through strong democratic participation for the common good, as other Americans have done from the 1770s until today. Or we might create new combinations of these ideas to seek new blends and balances in our quest to conjoin community and individuality in our constitutional order.

The wisdom of our choices will, to a great extent, depend on the quality of civic education available to all of our citizens. And our destiny as a people certainly will turn on the wisdom of our constitutional choices. So, systematic, ongoing, and challenging critical inquiry about the core ideas and issues of American constitutionalism is the ultimate imperative of civic education for democracy.

We must teach our students that our constitutional tradition is unfinished and imperfect. We must challenge them to continue the constitutional debates begun during the founding era toward the end of sustaining the best in our constitutional tradition and improving on the rest of it.[15]

## Notes

1. Herman Belz defines constitutionalism "as forms, principles, and procedures of limited government. Constitutionalism addresses the perennial problem of how to establish government with sufficient power to realize a community's shared purposes, yet so structured and controlled that oppression will be prevented" (Hall 1992, p. 190).
2. Richard C. Sinopoli (p. 131) emphasizes that "this consensus on deep ideological principles exists side by side with differences over

the desirability of certain institutions, policies, and civic character traits."

3. John Adams wrote *Thoughts on Government* to counter ideas about popular government and republicanism expressed by Thomas Paine in his 1776 booklet, *Common Sense*.

4. Publius was the collective pseudonym of the authors of *The Federalist*, Alexander Hamilton, James Madison, and John Jay. Brutus was the pseudonym of an unknown Anti-Federalist writer. Some scholars claim that Robert Yates of New York was Brutus.

5. See, for example, *West Virginia Board of Education* v. *Barnette*, 319 U.S. 624 (1943) and *United States* v. *O'Brien*, 391 U.S. 367 (1968). The *West Virginia* case is an example of limitations on majority rule to protect minority rights. The *O'Brien* case is an example of limitations on individual liberty on behalf of majority rule and the public good (Hall 1992, pp. 602, 925).

6. Both Anastaplo and Berns see the Constitution of 1787 as a fulfillment of the criteria for good government stated in the Declaration of Independence. Berns writes, "Somehow that Constitution did what the Declaration of Independence says must be done and what other constitutions have typically been unable to do: it instituted a government that secures human rights" (p. 121). Bernard Bailyn agrees with Berns in his celebrated work, *The Ideological Origins of the American Revolution*, see pages 321-81.

7. A copy of the Pennsylvania Constitution of 1776, with commentary, is presented in Bernard Schwartz, *The Roots of the Bill of Rights*, Vol. 2 (1980, pp. 262-75); a copy of the Massachusetts Constitution of 1780, with commentary, can be found in Stephen L. Schechter, *Roots of the Republic* (1990, pp. 188-226).

8. Brutus wrote, "[T]he people must give their assent to the laws by which they are governed. This is the true criterion between a free Government and an arbitrary one. The former are ruled by the will of the whole, expressed in any manner they may agree upon, the latter by the will of one or a few" (Storing 1981*b*, p. 114). The contrasting views of Publius can be examined in *Federalist* 10 and 51; in these two papers Publius (James Madison) explains how a "well-constructed Union" can be "a Republican remedy for the diseases most incident to Republican Government," such as majoritarian tyranny and inability to maintain social order to secure individual rights (Cooke 1961, p. 65).

9. The best edition of *The Federalist Papers* is edited by Jacob E. Cooke (1961); the best collection of Anti-Federalist papers in one volume is edited by Herbert J. Storing (1981*a*).

10. Storing claims that Brutus was the best of the Anti-Federalist writers in directly opposing the ideas of *The Federalist Papers*.

11. Both Galston and Macedo attempt to blend fundamental liberal constitutional concerns with communitarian commitments to the public good and civic virtue. In this effort, they appear to be faithful to James Madison's criteria for the pursuit of good government stated in *Federalist* 10.

12. Palmer treats the spread of democratic ideas in Western civilization. By contrast, our current age of democratic revolutions is global, as conceptualized and discussed in two new books: Joshua Muravchik, *Exporting Democracy: Fulfilling America's Destiny* (1992), and Theodore H. Von Laue, *The World Revolution of Westernization: The Twentieth Century in Global Perspective* (1987).

13. An excellent source of materials for debates on constitutional amendments is Alice O'Connor et al., *Rediscovering the Constitution: A Reader for Jefferson Meeting Debates* (1987); this volume contains materials for classroom debates on constitutional issues that have divided Americans from the founding era until the present, such as the desirability of term limits for members of Congress, direct election of the President, direct accountability of the U.S. Supreme Court to the people, a national referendum procedure, and so forth.

14. Gunnar Myrdal, the astute observer of political and social life in the United States, perceived the vitality and utility of the core civic ideas that he called an "American Creed" in his seminal work, *An American Dilemma*. Myrdal claimed that this "American Creed is the cement in the structure of this great and disparate nation" (1944, p. 4).

15. Donald Lutz (1988, pp. 167-70) reminds us that public debate on the meaning and practices of American constitutionalism is an unfinished and open-ended project. Lutz challenges us to confront and cope with "an unfinished constitutional tradition," which is rooted in the American founding era and its Colonial-era antecedents.

## References

Adams, John. "Thoughts on Government." In *Roots of the Republic: American Founding Documents Interpreted*, edited by Stephen L. Schechter. Madison, Wis.: Madison House, 1990.

Anastaplo, George. *The Constitution of 1787: A Commentary*. Baltimore: Johns Hopkins University Press, 1989.

Bailyn, Bernard. *The Ideological Origins of the American Revolution.* Cambridge, Mass.: Harvard University Press, 1992.

Barber, Benjamin R. *Strong Democracy: Participatory Politics for a New Age.* Berkeley: University of California Press, 1984.

Barber, Benjamin R. *An Aristocracy of Everyone: The Politics of Education and the Future of America.* New York: Ballantine, 1992.

Bellah, Robert N., et al. *The Good Society.* New York: Alfred A. Knopf, 1991.

Berns, Walter. *Taking the Constitution Seriously.* Lanham, Md.: Madison, 1992.

Butts, R. Freeman. *The Civic Mission in Educational Reform.* Stanford, Calif.: Hoover Institution Press, 1989.

Carey, George. *The Federalist: Design for a Constitutional Republic.* Urbana: University of Illinois Press, 1989.

Cooke, Jacob, ed. The Federalist *by Alexander Hamilton, James Madison, and John Jay.* Middleton, Conn.: Wesleyan University Press, 1961.

Diamond, Martin. *The Founding of the Democratic Republic.* Itasca, Ill.: F.E. Peacock, 1981.

Galston, William A. *Liberal Purposes: Goods, Virtues, and Diversity in the Liberal State.* New York: Cambridge University Press, 1991.

Hall, Kermit L., ed. *The Oxford Companion to the Supreme Court of the United States.* New York: Oxford University Press, 1992.

Ketchum, Ralph. *Framed for Posterity: The Enduring Philosophy of the Constitution.* Lawrence: University Press of Kansas, 1993.

Koch, Adrienne, ed. *Notes of Debates in the Federal Convention of 1787 Reported by James Madison.* New York: W.W. Norton, 1987.

Leming, James. "Research on Social Studies Curriculum and Instruction." In *Review of Research in Social Studies Education, 1976-1983*, edited by William B. Stanley. Washington, D.C.: National Council for the Social Studies, 1985.

Lutz, Donald S. *The Origins of American Constitutionalism.* Baton Rouge: Louisiana State Press, 1988.

Macedo, Stephen. *Liberal Virtues: Citizenship, Virtue, and Community in Liberal Constitutionalism.* New York: Oxford University Press, 1990.

Morgan, Edmund S. *The Birth of the Republic, 1763-1789.* Chicago: University of Chicago Press, 1977.

Morgan, Edmund S. *Inventing the People: The Rise of Popular Sovereignty in England and America.* New York: W.W. Norton, 1988.

Mullis, Ina, et al. *Accelerating Academic Achievement: A Summary of 20 Years of NAEP*. Princeton, N.J.: Educational Testing Service, 1990.

Muravchik, Joshua. *Exporting Democracy: Fulfilling America's Destiny*. Washington, D.C.: AEI Press, 1992.

Myrdal, Gunnar. *An American Dilemma*. New York: Harper & Brothers, 1944.

National Assessment of Educational Progress (NAEP). *The Civics Report Card*. Princeton, N.J.: Educational Testing Service, 1990.

O'Connor, Alice; Henze, Mary L.; and Merriman, W. Richard. *Rediscovering the Constitution: A Reader for Jefferson Meeting Debates*. Washington, D.C.: Congressional Quarterly, 1987.

Paine, Thomas. *Common Sense*, edited by Isaac Krammick. Middlesex, England: Penguin Books, 1976.

Palmer, R.R. *The Age of the Democratic Revolution, 1760-1800*. Princeton, N.J.: Princeton University Press, 1959.

Peterson, Paul. "Antifederalist Thought in Contemporary American Politics." In *Anti-Federalism*, edited by Josephine F. Pacheco. Fairfax, Va.: George Mason University Press, 1992.

Richards, David A.J. *Foundations of American Constitutionalism*. New York: Oxford University Press, 1989.

Schechter, Stephen L., ed. *Roots of the Republic: American Founding Documents Interpreted*. Madison, Wis.: Madison House, 1990.

Schwartz, Bernard, ed. *The Roots of the Bill of Rights*. 5 Vols. New York: Chelsea House, 1980.

Sinopoli, Richard C. *The Foundations of American Citizenship: Liberalism, the Constitution, and Civic Virtue*. New York: Oxford University Press, 1992.

Storing, Herbert J., ed. *The Anti-Federalist: Writings by the Opponents of the Constitution*. Chicago: University of Chicago Press, 1981. a

Storing, Herbert J. *What the Anti-Federalists Were For*. Chicago: University of Chicago Press, 1981. b

Sunstein, Cass R. "Constitutions and Democracies." In *Constitutionalism and Democracy*, edited by Jon Elster and Rune Slagstad. New York: Cambridge University Press, 1988.

Von Laue, Theodore H. *The World Revolution of Westernization: The Twentieth Century in Global Perspective*. New York: Oxford University Press, 1987.

# The Power of Comparison in Teaching About Democracy

## BY KERMIT L. HALL

H.G. Wells remarked that history is "a race between education and catastrophe." Today the latter often seems to be winning. Violence, intolerance, and ethnic conflict punctuate our national existence and plague other nations. We have a right, under such circumstances, to ask ourselves whether education has a role in solving the great problems of the modern age. The challenge, of course, is not new. Plato pondered 2,500 years ago the fact that while education can make people clever, it cannot make them good. And history is replete with examples of peoples and societies that were well-educated but evil. Nazi Germany comes immediately to mind. One of Adolph Hitler's chief lieutenants, Martin Borman, once explained that the only purpose of schools was to produce "useful coolies."[1] Joseph Stalin called education "a weapon whose effect depends on who holds it in his hands and at whom it is aimed."[2] What we teach, therefore, and how we teach it can make a substantial difference in the outcome of Wells' race.

There is no doubt that an important part of winning that race is forging a meaningful link between learning and civic responsibility. John Adams, in the wake of the ratification of this nation's constitution, observed that "liberty cannot be preserved without a general knowledge among the people."[3]

What should we be teaching in order to equip the next generation to become literate in constitutionalism, democracy, and the law?

We are not isolated in posing this question. We are part of a worldwide revolution in human rights, federalism, and civic education for democracy. Any recent reader of the international press appreciates that the wave of democratic reform sweeping the world has generated unprecedented interest in civic education. In nations as different as Haiti, Poland, the United Kingdom, Russia, Ukraine, and even China, civic education has become a high priority.[4] And if further evidence of interest is necessary, then we need look only to President Bill Clinton, who called for the establishment of a volunteer Democracy Corps to nurture democratic development through the promotion of civic education in nations emerging from communism and authoritarianism.

In the United States the ferment has reached a high pitch, so much so that consumer advocate Ralph Nader has come forward with a new how-to book on civic education, titled *Civics for Democracy: A Journey for Teachers and Students*.[5] Nader claims that the time for change has come in teaching civic education because the present curriculum is "built on dull, abstract principles" when it ought to engage students in activities such as energy surveys in their schools and to educate them in civic action techniques, including staging press conferences and using the Freedom of Information Act.[6]

Nader may or may not be right about his prescription for civic activism. That is not our concern here. Instead, his call for reform merely echoes other efforts, such as the *Civitas* project.[7] The time has arrived for a fresh look at the way in which we go about educating our students for democracy, and doing so is especially crucial given the resurgent interest in most of the rest of the world in that very subject.

What gives added urgency to this task is that we live in a time of unrelenting criticism of schools, of public education, of teacher performance, and of what our students understand about law and democracy, some of which Nader would doubtless describe as "dull, and abstract." We hear repeatedly of civic illiterates — of students who do not know enough to even know how to be good citizens. There must be a problem; everyone, it seems, is telling us that there is.

That problem exists in two dimensions. First, there is not enough teaching about issues of governance, law, and democracy. Second is Nader's charge that much of what is taught is anachronistic and dull. We might add to this list a charge of parochialism, which is rooted, at least partly, in the recently entombed Cold War.

We probably should not waste time quibbling about degrees of failure, though the picture seems a bit too stark to reflect accurately where we are and how we can improve. However, for the sake of argument, let us accept that we should do more teaching and concentrate on the second of these two shortcomings — what is taught or, to put the matter correctly, what is *not* taught.

There is a substantial content problem, though it is far more challenging than Nader would suppose. The state of teaching about constitutionalism, democracy, and law reflects not so much the inadequacies of the teachers as shortcomings in the way they are prepared to teach these subjects, especially historical matters. In most universities the history of law and legal institutions has taken a back seat to social history, with its emphasis on history from the bottom up, its attention to ethno-cultural, gender, and race issues, and its concern for informal rather than formal means of social control. If current debates about the need to devote greater attention to ethnicity and race in the schools are any indication, there is little reason to believe that we are likely to see, without some real efforts, more attention devoted to constitutionalism and liberty as important subjects for would-be teachers.

While many constitutional and legal historians view the ascendancy of social history as a threat, such a reaction is unwarranted on intellectual and pragmatic grounds. The law, legal processes, and legal institutions should be a part of the social history of America. But the sad fact is that we are not equipping teachers with an integrated view of either. University history departments and colleges of education have some responsibility in this matter, but they have done a poor job of fulfilling it. Social history and constitutional/legal history are reciprocal and reinforcing; that is the way in which teachers should learn about them. Such an approach also is one of the best ways of demonstrating to students the important lesson that the study of law and the study of society go together.

111

The history of the Bill of Rights and the Constitution, as Nader correctly observes, have for too long been treated as subjects dealing with bearded white men sitting on a distant national court. Do not mistake me; these justices and their Supreme Court have been important. However, we should do more to stretch the traditional boundaries of law and constitutionalism so that teachers learn about the history of "rights consciousness," "distributive justice," and "total justice," to invoke some of the phrases associated with the so-called new legal history.[8] In sum, until history departments and schools of education offer teachers an integrated view of social and legal history, we are unlikely to be able to make a convincing case that, in the zero-sum game of education, more resources should be directed to instruction about the Constitution, law, and democracy.

Promoting change also will mean rethinking the conceptual base that informs what is taught. What is most important in teaching about the Constitution, law, and democracy is not their content but their meaning and value. Nader is right: We should equip our students to be *effective* as well as affective citizens. Yet we also should remember — as Nader seems not to — that meaningful social action always is rooted in a clear understanding of the principles (invariably abstract principles) at play in any social situation. There is a difference, of course, between teaching dull principles and dully teaching important principles.

In a world of democratic revolutions the question is, How do we accomplish this goal? Instead of issuing a laundry list of recommendations, let us concentrate on one concrete suggestion. Whether from a historical or contemporary political science/civics/law-related education perspective, we need to broaden the scope of what is taught to include specific comparisons between the American federal system of law and constitutionalism and its counterparts in the states and other nations.[9] The task before us is not just to "globalize" our teaching, though that is certainly an important part of the task. We also need to push our students — who will work, live, and compete in the global village — to appreciate, once again, that law is a system of social choice and that different cultures have and do make different choices.

What are the virtues of a comparative approach? It offers three broadly overlapping purposes or functions. First and most basic, comparison creates an awareness of alternatives, showing developments to be significant that without a comparative perspective might not appear so. Second, comparison as a teaching method serves as a primitive form of "experimentation." The approach allows students to test the relative impact of various social, economic, demographic, political, or intellectual factors on the form of different nations' civic cultures. Third, the comparative approach also allows students to identify common patterns of action and behavior. For example, comparisons can teach our students about the vagaries of our federal system, while also breaking down the parochialism that has clothed much teaching about civics since World War II.

The comparative approach should start at home. Bear in mind that we teach little about the national constitutional and legal order; we do even less to explain state and local developments. Most teachers, we might conjecture, simply are not equipped to deal with the shift from state-based to nationally centered federalism. Yet the experience of the states in organizing government and distributing and protecting rights has been crucial. State constitutions and state bills of rights historically have filled the gaps created by our incomplete federal Constitution. The federal document is largely unintelligible without reference to the state documents and, as important, comparisons between federal and state experiences and practices offer an excellent starting point for a general appreciation of constitutional government.

State bills of rights provided the model for the federal Bill of Rights. State constitutions are the oldest continuous source of constitutional government in the world, with the Massachusetts Constitution of 1780 being the earliest. Until quite recently, however, these state bills of rights and constitutions had faded in importance. In their place, the federal Bill of Rights and national protection of liberty had become far more important. One of the reasons that the state bills of rights faded in importance was that they, like the constitutions of the Third World that I will discuss shortly, increasingly became codes of law rather than fundamental frames of government. The average state constitution is about 27,000 words long. The U.S. Constitution is about 7,500 words long, even with its 27 amendments; only Vermont has a shorter constitution. While there has been only one federal constitutional convention, there have be more than 230 state conventions and more than 8,500 amendments made to these documents. In short, state constitutions have become *super legislation*, promising through constitutional law that which could not be attained through the regular legislative process.[10]

Recently, state constitutions and their associated bills of rights have gone through a renaissance, a new federalism. With the due-process revolution of the Warren Court era at an end, civil rights lawyers have turned to the state documents to raise the ceiling of liberty above the floor created by the federal Bill of Rights.[11] This "new federalism" is expanding the scope of all of our rights, yet few teachers and students know practically anything about these developments.

We also can profitably search for comparisons beyond our own borders. We need to remember that different cultures do have different ways of going about making social choices through the law. This insight is especially important because there is a revolution under way, and once again we are ill-prepared to deal with it — even though doing so would place our scheme of governance in sharp relief. During the last two decades a worldwide renaissance in federalism and individual rights has occurred. There have been sweeping efforts at constitutional reforms in Canada, India, Nigeria, Switzerland, Australia, and, most recently, Eastern Europe and the former Soviet Union.[12] We are not the only nation on earth to have either a written constitution or a bill of rights, yet we invariably teach about both as if that were the case.[13]

Our nation is one of the few in the world to rely on judicial interpretation of a relatively brief constitutional text as a means of protecting individual rights. Such a practice means that we have considerably more lawyers and place a substantially greater premium on the adversarial process than does a country like Japan, for example. They have one lawyer for every 9,000 people; we have one lawyer for every 235 people. By 1995 we will have one million lawyers in the United States. Depending on where you are on the political spectrum, this bounty of lawyers is either a disaster or a necessary condition to accommodate unprecedented racial, gender, economic, and technological change sweeping our society.[14] What the figures reveal, in any case, is that it is a distinctly — indeed, almost a uniquely — American response to broader issues that beset the entire planet.

Much of the explanation for this uniqueness stems from the American approach to rights. Historically, we have placed tremendous weight on individual rights rather than group rights. As a result, we have turned to courts and lawyers to pursue and defend those rights. Most countries of the developing world and of socialized industrial nations have taken a significantly different approach, one in which they have developed *social constitutions*. These documents not only give different weight to individual and group rights, but they also are considerably longer than the American federal Constitution.

For example, one might consider the social constitutions of the Philippines, Nigeria, and Brazil. The governing documents of those countries offer extensive written guarantees to economic rights, equality for different ethnic groups, and rights of the urban poor. The Philippine Constitution, for example, declares "Filipino" to be the official language; and it obliges government to promote agrarian land reform, equality for women, better family life, free public education, health care, and urban housing. It even provides that each person has a right to participate in sports that the government is duty-bound to promote.

Documents such as the constitution of the Philippines contrast sharply with our Bill of Rights, which makes only broad promises and makes those promises legally, not politically, enforceable. In essence, countries around the world are attempting to use social constitutions for the purpose of radical reform — they seek through their declarations or bills of rights *to invent* as well as *to interpret* society. Consequently, these documents tend to be quite lengthy.

Nigeria's constitution has 279 articles; Brazil's has more than 400; and the Philippines' has almost 200 articles.

Moreover, in each of these countries, the judiciary remains relatively weak, a condition that contrasts sharply with the American experience. In many countries the power of the judiciary to interpret the constitution is frustrated by military force, by an aggressive legislature, or by a system of government organization that does not allow for what is "legal" to be conclusive in matters of political dispute.

An interesting variant is the place of the Charter of Rights in Canada. That nation's new constitution grafted a Charter of Rights and Freedoms and judicial review onto a federal parliamentary system. But that constitution contains a novel provision, Section 33, which permits parliament to suspend major individual rights for up to five years. Section 33 states: "Parliament or the legislature of a province may expressly declare in an Act of Parliament or of the legislature . . . that the Act or a provision thereof shall operate notwithstanding a provision included in" the Charter's provisions dealing with fundamental freedoms, legal rights, and equality rights.[15] These declarations can be in effect for no longer than five years, the maximum period a government can exist without going to the people in an election campaign. However, they can be renewed indefinitely.

Section 33 creates a set of circumstances in Canadian constitutional law far different from that in the United States. To begin with, the provision means that parliament can checkmate the judiciary should it believe that the judges are getting out of control (becoming an imperial force, for example). As important is the fact that this section demonstrates that even within the Anglo-American legal orbit, rights can appear in strong, but not absolute, form.[16]

Section 33 also creates within the Canadian constitutional system an opportunity for the courts and the legislature to engage in a unique dialogue. One of the chief causes of the debilitation of democratic governments is the truncated nature of such discussions. However, in the Canadian system the opportunity exists for a deliberative judicial consideration of a difficult and perhaps divisive constitutional issue *and* an opportunity for electorally accountable officials to respond in the course of ordinary politics.[17] At the same time, the framers of the new charter have provided that both the right to vote and the right to be educated in English or French are exempt from this "override" provision.[18]

What all of this adds up to is that the American scheme of rights, as set forth in the majestic generalities of the Bill of Rights, is unique because of the great reliance it places on judicial review and protection of those rights. The social constitutions of much of the rest of the world are not merely wordy; they guarantee too much without the legal, economic, and political wherewithal to fulfill those promises. When promises go unfulfilled, people lose faith not only in government but also in the idea of constitutionalism itself. Recent events in Eastern Europe make us appreciate the difficulty that political leaders there face in making rights a legal as well as a political reality.

That we do not have social constitutions tells us much about the advantages, as well as the limitations, of our scheme of rights and our practice of protecting those rights through the continuing constitutional convention that we call the Supreme Court. The power of comparison in history always is telling, and an especially strong case can be made for such an approach in teaching about constitutionalism and rights rather than just about the Constitution and the Bill of Rights.

A comparative approach also is helpful because it affirms that there was nothing inevitable about the outcome of the controversies that produced our current constitutional and legal order. At any one of several points, events could have taken a different turn. Equally important, it is essential for our students to understand that other countries have, when confronted with the same set of circumstances, decided to make social choices quite different from ours. Consider, for example, the matter of hate speech.

Why has law and policy in the United States developed in a different direction from virtually every other country in the world? Most countries prohibit the expression of offensive racial, religious, or ethnic propaganda. According to Human Rights Watch, "The United States stands virtually alone in having no valid statutes penalizing expression that is offensive or insulting on such grounds as race, religion or ethnicity."[19] A report by Article 19, a London-based anti-censorship organization, concluded that on this issue the world could be divided into "the United States and the rest." In the former, it reported, "The balance is unequivocally drawn in favor of freedom of speech."[20]

The following examples demonstrate how exceptional the American response to hate speech has been.

- The 1986 Public Order Act in the United Kingdom makes it a crime to use threatening, abusive, or insulting words or behavior with respect to color, race, nationality (including citizenship) or ethnic or national origins.
- The constitution of Brazil declares that propaganda relating to religious, race, or class prejudice shall not be tolerated.
- In Turkey a person faces a prison term of one to three years for publicly inciting people to hatred and enmity on the basis of class, race, religion, sect, or region.[21]

Germany has a specific law allowing any victim of the Holocaust to bring a legal action against anyone who denies that the Holocaust occurred.[22] Closer to home, the Canadian Charter of Rights and Freedoms balances a guarantee of freedom of expression with the proviso that "reasonable limits" on individual rights may be justified. The Canadian Supreme Court used this rationale to sustain the criminal conviction of a teacher who made anti-Semitic remarks in the classroom.[23] This list of examples, by the way, does not include the several important international human rights declarations, such as the 1966 International Covenant on Civil and Political Rights, that go even further in calling for limitations on offensive speech.[24]

The institutional arrangements by which different cultures protect rights offers another powerful point of comparison. The American system of rights relies heavily on courts and judges to protect basic rights. Judicial review is the practice by which courts review the actions of legislative and executive bodies to determine whether they correspond with basic constitutional precepts. In the past two centuries the scope and character of judicial review has grown enormously, especially in the American Supreme Court. Its nine justices, appointed during good behavior and subject to removal only through impeachment and conviction, enjoy an extraordinary degree of independence from the political process. The Court is almost exclusively a legal body, one that hears and decides cases. In the American system, the Supreme Court provides for a system of concrete review of legislation after it has been enacted into law.[25]

However, other nations have settled on schemes of judicial review and court organization far different from those in the United States. The model of judicial review in these countries is "diffuse," enabling these countries to exercise such review only in genuine "cases and controversies" where parties have established "standing." In such cases, trial court judgments may be reviewed by appellate tribunals, with the Supreme Court having final judgment. Countries with such systems — many with common-law backgrounds — include a number of Latin American nations, Greece, Australia, Canada, Japan, India, Pakistan, Burma, and most Scandinavian nations. Germany, France, Spain, and Italy have a more "concentrated" mode of review wherein a specific court or courts, sometimes separate from the regular judicial system, resolve constitutional questions. Some of these nations have more relaxed requirements for standing than do American courts, to the extent of permitting advisory opinions and a strong degree of political influence in the decision-making process.

In France, for example, the Gaullist constitution of 1958 established the French Constitutional Council. The council was designed primarily to ensure that parliament would not undermine the important powers given by that constitution to the president. Unlike the American Supreme Court, the French Constitutional Council is an expressly political body. It has nine members who serve nine-year, nonrenewable terms. The president of France, the president of the Senate, and the president of the National Assembly each name three members.[26] Unlike the modern American Supreme Court, the French council has been dominated by politicians, especially former ministers of the French government. In 1986, for example, eight of the council's nine members had been ministers.

The French council exercises its powers in a manner that is much different from its American counterpart. Its review is *a priori* and abstract; that is, the council acts before a case is brought and it does so based on theoretical — abstract — concerns about the appropriateness of the legislation rather than a concrete case in which a party sues claiming some real injury. The council reviews laws after their adoption by the parliament but before their official promulgation. The nation's leading political figures — the president, the prime minister, the presidents of the branches of parliament — may invoke judicial review by referring laws to the council, as may the sixty members of either branch of parliament.

Although very different from its American counterpart, this highly political form of judicial review has proved more than capable of protecting the rights of French citizens. For example, the Socialist government elected in France in 1981 sought, among other things, to carry out an extensive nationalization of the economy and to break up existing media monopolies. However, the council, dominated by Gaullist appointees, rejected both efforts. On 16 January 1982 the council held that major aspects of the Socialist nationalization program violated a constitutional principle embedded in the 1789 Declaration of Rights against taking property without just compensation.[27] The council also thwarted the Socialist efforts to end the hold of media monopolies over the distribution of news in France. Parliament effectively outlawed one monopoly, owned by a former Nazi collaborator, Robert Hersant, and prevented it from re-forming in the future. But the council, while sustaining the government's legislation in principle, rejected its particular application to existing media groups, including that of Hersant.[28]

The advantages of such comparisons are manifold. First, it is important, at least where matters of judicial review, hate speech, and civil discourse are involved, that we appreciate how unique we are. Teachers of American history and culture have long wrestled with the question of American exceptionalism. We know what we are by knowing how others are different or alike. In the case of hate speech, the American response is genuinely unique, but it also is a dramatic affirmation of how much stock we put in individual expression, the ways in which that emphasis deeply complicates our race relations, and how such basic instincts are transmitted through law and legal institutions. Indeed, we might consider hate speech, when viewed in that way, as one of the "costs" of a constitutional democracy. For some, at least, this cost is a dramatic manifestation of the darker side of our emphasis on protecting individual rights through the law.

In the case of judicial review, we should recognize that the American approach is only one way of invalidating the actions of government as unconstitutional. Even in countries similar to the United States, where judicial review is firmly rooted, we should remember that disputes can arise about how freely such review should be exercised. In other countries, the process of constitutional change has moved through the amending process, with judges playing a minor and often political role.

Second, such comparisons begin to move our students and their teachers toward giving real meaning to the concepts of globalization, internationalization, and multiculturalism. In the last few years we have given considerable attention to the ways in which the American economy functions in the international marketplace. The new economic literacy, to coin a phrase, is distinctly cross-cultural and multinational. So, too, must be the new democratic literacy. We must cease to think parochially about our scheme of governance, about constitutionalism, about rights, and about law if we are to become fully competitive. There is, in the end, a far richer, more complex, and ultimately more challenging vision of who we are as a people if we are willing to take account of how we compare with other people in other places who are trying to make the same social choices.

Third, the inherent cosmopolitanism of a comparative approach holds the additional promise of elevating the entire educational experience, for both teachers and students. We cannot pretend any longer to be educated people and learn about others only through our own language. The end of the Cold War not only has liberated us from the military-industrial complex but also has given us the opportunity to appreciate others on their terms, rather than on ours.

All of this talk of comparisons, either internal or external, may strike some readers as so much pie in the sky. We cannot get our students to understand the American system, the argument runs, let alone that of another country — even one so close in language, culture, and geography as Canada. One might argue that the absence of a comparative dimension in teaching about constitutionalism, law, and democracy may well explain why students neither appreciate nor understand their own system as well as they might. We tend to understand best that for which we have a reference point. Thus what on first impression might seem to be a merely clever approach may be, in fact, quite fundamental.

Leaving aside questions of how to teach comparatively, we must recognize that using comparisons raises inherent value choices — and raises the hackles of some observers as well. After all, any student exposed to the way in which hate speech is treated in the rest of world might appropriately ask whether American exceptionalism in this matter is a good thing. Of course, that is exactly what we should be doing with our students: challenging them to think critically about our system of governance and law. The specter of the "Red Menace" has lifted; we may even find that others have a better way of proceeding in certain matters, such as hate speech. Even if we discover that our present arrangements are the best of the lot, we may find that some students gain an increased fidelity to them simply because they have critically explored other possibilities.

In conclusion, two proposals come to mind: one modest, the other radical. The modest proposal is that we encourage teachers to couple the current emphasis on multiculturalism to a broadened vision of cross-cultural and international studies of law and law-related subjects. We do not have to overhaul the curriculum to do so; we simply need teachers who understand that at certain key points in teaching about "our" system of constitutionalism, law, and democracy they can actually achieve more by teaching less about "us" and more about "them."

The more radical proposal is to shift conceptual gears entirely in teaching these subjects and to adopt a strongly thematic and value-based approach that works less on having students understand our system and more on having them appreciate the values embodied in that system. Hence, any examination of American governance would necessarily raise the question for students of whether absolute free speech is desirable. That discussion would necessarily take place in a comparative dimension, one in which students learn that other cultures weigh ends and means differently from how ours does, that they organize to protect rights differently, and that, consequently, they produce a civic culture and a social order that may be more or less desirable than ours.

This more radical approach, of course, would require a radical redesign of teaching materials, a more open and accepting approach to the world around us, and a sophisticated new undergraduate curriculum for future teachers of government, civics, and law in K-12 education.

Under either proposal, we need to affirm that the history of American legal culture is the history of concepts, ideas, and values — they are Nader's dull, abstract principles. What we so often miss, however, is that these principles will take on greater meaning when viewed in comparative perspective. Our legal history is one of human choices and decisions, some made for good, others for ill. What students need to grasp is that, as a nation, we long ago committed ourselves to the idea of the rule of law and of limited government and to a scheme of rights protected through law and safeguarded by judicial power. Hence, students need to know something of the ideas that inform the history of the Constitution as well as the structures through which competing constitutional claims — by government and by individuals — have been lawfully reconciled. The framing of the Constitution, the creation of the Bill of Rights, and the subsequent development of both have importance not in and of themselves but as they reveal to us how well (and not so well) they have performed in distributing social costs, allocating power, and granting benefits and rewards.

The passing of the Cold War and the decline of communism is a wonderful moment to reach out and understand the rest of the world. The comparative approach promises to do what is essential: to help our students appreciate that all law is a system of social choice, that such choices are conditioned by underlying social and cultural assumptions, and that understanding the relationship between social systems and legal regimes is important.

As H.G. Wells reminded us, history is a race between education and catastrophe. The value of a comparative approach in this contest is to increase the accuracy of our knowledge about constitutionalism, law, and democracy. In so doing, we help our students to make better-informed choices at home as they become better informed about the diverse alternatives to our system that exist throughout our ever-shrinking world.

## Notes

1. Barry James, "UNESCO Panel to Ponder the Challenge to Education of Creating a New Humanism," *International Herald Tribune* , 17 February 1993, p. 1.
2. Ibid.
3. Ibid.
4. See, for example, *International Herald Tribune*, 17 February 1993; *British Broadcasting Corporation: Summary of World Broadcasts*, 4 January 1993; and *South China Morning Post*, 17 December 1992.
5. Washington, D.C.: Essential Books, 1993.
6. Ralph Nader, as quoted in *Sacramento Bee*, 4 December 1992.
7. Charles F. Bahmueller, ed., *Civitas: A Framework for Civic Education* (Calabasas, Calif.: Center for Civic Education, 1991).
8. See, for example, Kermit L. Hall, *The Magic Mirror: Law in American History* (New York: Oxford University Press, 1990), pp. 330-31, 333-36.
9. *The ACLS Comparative Constitutionalism Project: Final Report, ACLS Occasional Paper No. 13* (New York: American Council of Learned Societies, 1990).

10. Kermit L. Hall, "Mostly Anchor and Little Sail: The Evolution of American State Constitutions," in *Toward a Usable Past: Liberty Under State Constitutions*, edited by Paul Finkelman and Stephen E. Gottlieb (Athens: University of Georgia Press, 1991), pp. 388-418.

11. Kermit L. Hall, "Floors and Ceilings: The New Federalism and State Bills of Rights," in *The Bill of Rights in Modern America: After 200 Years*, edited by David J. Bodenhamer and James W. Ely, Jr. (Bloomington: Indiana University Press, 1993), pp. 191-206.

12. See, for example, E.L. Roy Hunt, "Human Rights in a New World Order," *Florida Journal of International Law* 6 (Fall 1990): 1-4.

13. Louis Henkin and Albert J. Rosenthal, eds., *Constitutionalism and Rights: The Influence of the United States Constitution Abroad* (New York: Columbia University Press, 1990).

14. Lawrence M. Friedman, *Total Justice* (New York: Russell Sage Foundation, 1985), pp. 7-10.

15. Canadian Constitution (Constitution Act, 1982), pt. 1 (Canadian Charter of Rights and Freedoms), Section 33.

16. Mary Ann Glendon, *Rights Talk: The Impoverishment of Political Discourse* (Cambridge, Mass.: Harvard University Press, 1991), p. 39.

17. Michael Perry, "The Constitution, the Courts, and the Question of Minimalism," *Northwestern University Law Review* 88 (1993): 158.

18. Paul Weiler, "Rights and Judges in a Democracy: A New Canadian Version," *University of Michigan Journal of Law Reform* 18 (1984): 65.

19. Human Rights Watch, *"Hate Speech" and Freedom of Expression: A Human Rights Watch Policy Paper* (New York: Human Rights Watch, March 1992), p. 7. There are, of course, many laws on the books; but they would stand little chance of passing constitutional scrutiny in light of *R.A.V.* v. *City of St. Paul*, 60 U.S.L.W. 4667 (June 22, 1992).

20. Kevin Boyle, "Overview of a Dilemma: Censorship Versus Racism," in *Striking a Balance: Hate Speech, Freedom of Expression and Non-Discrimination*, edited by Sandra Coliver (London: Article 19, 1992), p. 4.

21. Ibid.

22. Eric Stein, "History Against Free Speech: The New German Law Against 'Auschwitz' — and other 'Lies'," *Michigan Law Review* 85 (November 1986): 277-324.

23. Kathleen Mahoney, "The Constitutional Approach to Freedom of Expression in Hate Propaganda and Pornography," *Law and Contemporary Problems* 55 (Winter 1992): 77-105.
24. For a comprehensive collection see Ian Brownlie, ed., *Basic Documents of Human Rights*, 2nd ed. (Oxford: Clarendon Press, 1981).
25. Kermit L. Hall, *The Supreme Court and Judicial Review in American History* (Washington, D.C.: American Historical Association, 1989).
26. Alec Stone, "The Judicialization of Politics," *International Political Science Review* 15 (1994): 1-19.
27. Ibid., p. 150.
28. Ibid., p. 190.

# PART III

# Other Societies, Other Problems

# Democracy and Education in Central and Eastern Europe

## BY WOLFGANG MITTER

The radical sociopolitical changes at the end of the 1980s laid the ground for the comprehensive transformation process with which Eastern Europe has been confronted. The effects of these changes on the education systems became manifest soon after the breakdown of the totalitarian regimes. In Hungary — with her gliding advance toward democracy — the effects had been introduced at the beginning of the 1980s (Kozma 1989); in Poland there has been a comparable trend since the "Solidarnosc" movement (1980-81) that strongly shocked the coherence of the social-ist system, which the resulting martial law was not able to restore (Kozakiewicz 1992; Kupisiewicz 1991).

## The Transformation Process as Framework

In the education system the revolutionary awakening was demonstrated by the banishment of Marxist-Leninist instruction from schools and universities, by the election of new rectors and deans at the universities and new school inspectors and head teachers at primary and secondary schools, and by the extinction of Marxist-Leninist and antidemocratic doctrines in syllabi and textbooks. These more or less spontaneous initiatives were accompanied by various kinds of pilot projects at the grassroots level of schools and communities, including the reorganization of structures within the education system and the introduction of curricular innovations, for example, in the fields of history and foreign languages.

At the margins of the innovative spectrum was the establishment of private schools and other forms of nongovernment education institutions.

Today it seems that the original élan has gone, giving way to widespread disenchantment. It is true that throughout Eastern and Central Europe new laws affecting education have been passed by national parliaments, though most have been transitory decisions, as frequently becomes evident soon after their enactment. These legal activities have been supported by government decrees that, in many cases, served as interim laws because legislative procedures often were delayed by unstable political conditions. Yet high expectations of short-term reforms have turned out to be premature or even illusory. Many early innovative pilot projects became stuck and so have given way to instructional and educational practices that only a short time previously had been relegated to the past.

Exaggerating the gloomy shadows of anti-reform indolence would be erroneous. Foreign observers find evidence of teachers' commitment and students' aspirations amidst counter-productive conditions in the schools. However, such observations are too casual to invalidate the overall gloomy picture.

Education, on the whole, has been dragged into the crisis that has seized the socioeconomic and political stage in the entire region of Eastern Europe. Schools are considered the most defenseless targets of austerity policies that result, among other deficiencies, in neglect of equipment, closing down of educational units (particularly preschools), dismissal of teachers, and poor remuneration for those educators who remain. In response to austerity policies, the teachers resort to various forms of passive resistance or even active resistance, such as strikes. On the other hand, the youngsters react to such measures with indifference, frustration, cynicism, or aggressiveness. Some young people drop out of school, expecting to make quick money on the free market.

The changes in Eastern European education are far from uniform across the various countries and regions. But they are part of an overarching socioeconomic, political, and cultural transformation process. Eastern Europe, as it previously existed, is disintegrating. The pretended monolithic character of the former socialist bloc was more an ideological slogan than a sociopolitical reality. It is this component of the transformation process that needs closer observation, because it will have an immediate influence on education policies and developments (Anweiler 1990, 1992; Bachmeier 1991; Górnikowska-Zwolak and Radziewicz-Winnicki 1992; Mitter, Weiss, and Schaefer 1992; Phillips and Kaser 1992; Svecová 1992).

Disintegration has affected the education systems in several ways. First, the emergence of *self-determined education policies* is a significant manifestation of national awakening, revival, or consolidation. Both the removal of Soviet dominance and intervention and the constitution of independent education systems inside the former Soviet Union have opened the door to reforms based on national principles and codified by legal and administrative measures. These changes have affected school management and supervision. Scope and effect, on the one hand, depend on the stability of the decision-making bodies and the rank that education issues are given in the political arena. On the other hand, they also reflect attitudes among the public, particularly those expressed by opinion leaders in professional associations and the media. In this latter context, debates about education goals and projects proposed by political parties or social organizations are important indicators of the state of affairs, all the more so because they also indicate the degree of democratization and pluralism that individual postsocialist societies have achieved.

Second, the path to democracy and to democratic citizenship is closely connected with how the new regimes cope with the establishment of *economic orders based on the free-market principle*. This principle has become the main incentive, if not a panacea, for overcoming the bankruptcy of socialist planning everywhere in the postsocialist region. However, devising free-market policies and implementing them depends on prerequisites, such as material provisions of the economic system and favorable attitudes and abilities of investors, employers, and employees. In this context the quality of the education systems plays an essential role. In particular, vocational education and inservice training (at various levels) are key. Policymakers' know-how and the general market-oriented attitude of the public are essential indicators of whether, how, and to what degree free-market strategies can be put into practice. Moreover, these factors influence political decisions, as has been demonstrated by the partition of Czechoslovakia.

Third, the radical political changes have encouraged the revival of *nation states built on the principle of ethnic nationhood* and on one national language to be used exclusively, or at least predominantly, in public and official communication. Education is affected by this principle, at least at the level of higher education. The monopolizing position of a national language is associated with cultural patterns that lead students to acceptance of and commitment to a defined national identity. The fact that in all the countries of Central and Eastern Europe this political concept collides with the existence of ethnic or religious minorities, with their vernaculars and cultural peculiarities and value patterns, seemed to be neglected as a source of growing tensions and conflicts in the years of "socialist euphoria." In fact, these matters are directly interrelated with the targets, contents, and methods of intercultural education and, moreover, education for democracy in general.

The diversity of the transformation process, taken as a whole, can be traced to the different national and regional traditions as expressed in the deliberations of policymakers and educators and in public debates. Particular attention must be paid to how, in each case, the national inheritance is related to the goal manifest in cross-national calls for a return to Europe and to a Western orientation in general. (I shall deal more with this issue in a moment.)

Granted the distinctiveness of each national case, it seems reasonable to classify their diversity in terms of a working concept. Here the main criterion is in the existing demarcation lines among regions.

The first region consists of the states of East Central Europe: the Czech Republic, Slovakia, Hungary, and Poland (Baske 1990*a*; Báthory 1990; Halász and Lukács 1990; Horváth and Mihály 1990; Kozakiewicz 1992; Kozma 1990; Nagy 1992; Pachocinski

1992; Prucha 1992; Prucha and Walterova 1992). They have made considerable and reasonably successful efforts in stabilizing pluralism and democracy. All of them definitely advocate and develop free-market policies and have reached fairly balanced relations between the principle of one-state nation and tolerance toward their ethnic minorities. Compared with the other regions, education policies in this region seem to be rather steady. For the time being there is still uncertainty in this matter regarding the Baltic Republics with their considerable Russian and Polish minorities, though their place in East Central Europe has never been questioned in principle (Dienys 1992; Rajangu 1993). But the placement in this region of Slovenia, with a traditional Austrian orientation, can be debated (Strajn 1992).

The second region is represented by Southeast Europe, which has been driven into a period of utmost turbulence and even chaos. It seems that the centuries-old boundary demarcating the Catholic from the Orthodox nations and nationalities has been revived; and the existence of Muslim populations — particularly in former Yugoslavia, as well as in Albania and Bulgaria — adds a further component to the multicultural and multinational diversity. It is true that the transformation process has been most drastically interrupted in former Yugoslavia by the outbreak of violence, war, and ethnic cleansing. Considering national cohesion and, above all, economic standards, Romania, Bulgaria, and Albania also have enormous obstacles on their paths ahead.

There can be no doubt that the third region, taken as a whole, is characterized by the widest range of internal diversity and uncertainty, which the state of education clearly reveals: the Commonwealth of Independent States (CIS), which is the successor of the Soviet Union (the Baltic Republics and, in legal terms, Georgia excluded). The past ten years have confirmed the peculiarity of this region with regard to its place in Eastern Europe and, furthermore, in the "European House," to use Mikhail Gorbachev's phrase from the days of *perestroika* (Baske 1990*b*; Davydov and Nikandrov 1991; Dunstan 1992; Gershunskij 1992; Gershunskij and Pullin 1990; Muckle 1990; Yarmachenko 1992).

This question has a long history, dating from the Middle Ages and, in its modern version, from Peter the Great. In the 19th and 20th centuries the idea of including Russians, Ukrainians, Belorussians, Georgians, and Armenians in the wider range of European nations was continually discussed by natives and foreigners and has now gained current significance. As far as the Russians are concerned, the passionate debates between the Zapadniki (Westerners) and Slavjanofili (Slavophils) provide an apt example of the endurance and intensity of this issue. Moreover, the multinational (and multicultural) composition of the CIS complicates its European option in view of its Asian nations and nationalities and its cohesion as a whole.

## The Historical Departure

The collapse of the socialist regimes in Eastern Europe and the Soviet Union has opened the door to a sociopolitical order based on the values of human rights, tolerance, and democracy. However, recent developments have given manifold evidence of the enormous obstacles lying in the way of this transformation. Indirectly, they flare up in a chapter of *Summer Meditations* by Vaclav Havel, in which the author writes about the relation between politics and moral practice. Havel was president of the Czechoslovak Republic between 1989 and 1992 and later was elected president of the Czech Republic. His words are worth quoting, because they directly call for education analysis and action:

> The return of freedom into a society, in which all moral standards were entirely dissolved, has led to the explosion of all kinds of evil human attitudes. Although it seems that this was inevitable and therefore to be expected, the extent is, in a disproportional way, greater than any one among us could have imagined before. It seems that the various problematic or at least ambiguous human inclinations, inconspicuously cherished in the society over years and, at the same time, inconspicuously included in the services of the day-to-day

134

course of a totalitarian system, have been suddenly liberated from this strait-jacket and thereby reached its full display in the end. The definite order — if one can define it as such — given them by the authoritarian regime (which thereby legalized it), has collapsed, but a new order which defines these attitudes, instead of utilizing them, namely an order of freely accepted responsibility to the whole and for the whole, has not emerged yet and cannot have done so, because such a responsibility grows in the course of many years and must be cultivated. (Havel 1992, pp. 125-26)

The role of education in this transformation process is restricted compared with the efforts to be made on the economic, social, political, and cultural scenes. On the other hand, its role must not be underestimated, all the more so because it is the basic tool for the return of freedom in the long run. Education for democracy has to cope with the socialist inheritance. Under the socialist regime it was considered part of the overall Marxist-Leninist doctrine, focused on the new man as the center of the predicted communist society (Baske 1990c; Mitter 1978; Phillips and Kaser 1992). This predicted figure was conceived as a human being having overcome alienation and having harmonized individual integrity and collective responsibility. Love of labor and communist brotherhood were considered to be essentials in this concept.

However, according to the Marxist-Leninist doctrines, the socialist society was the transitional stage to communism. Thus, in that stage, governments and people had to make compromises with the continuing existence of capitalist habits, taking into special consideration the permanent struggle against the outside capitalist West. These compromises became manifest in the high esteem in which socialist patriotism was held. The appreciation and remuneration of individual achievements in the production sphere — and in education — also must be mentioned in this context.

On the one hand, the schools in the socialist countries were places of education and upbringing in which the virtues of the new man were anticipated, such as intrinsic learning, love of work, and collective behavior. On the other hand, schools were defined as institutions aiming at achievement, whose diplomas indicated professional qualification (on the various levels right up to graduation from higher education and qualifying diplomas in the tertiary sphere of education) and status in society. This problem showed in particular that the principle of achievement, linked with rates of economic growth and material and ideological privileges, was employed explicitly as a stimulus to economic development and control of education. From this point of view, examinations could be seen as indicators of the value of the principle of achievement.

According to the official ideological interpretations, such compromises should be reached by voluntary acceptance among the socialist citizens. In the reality, however, conflicts were inevitable from the beginning. Such conflicts were either common to all socialist countries or came to light in specific forms (ranging from authoritarian to totalitarian practices) and within specific socio-economic and political spheres. The effects of these conflicts on education goals, contents, methods, and pedagogic styles resulted in a concept of education based on indoctrination and discipline, which external critics have called "command education." In this context, however, one must carefully study the internal diversity of the socialist bloc with regard to the presocialist inheritance of the individual countries. This is why the return of freedom turns up in different constellations. The nature of a country's democratic traditions plays an essential role in how and to what extent the return of freedom can operate.

With special regard to the countries of East Central Europe, views have been expressed that socialist education had been a failure from its start. This opinion is rooted in solid ground, insofar as today's revolutionary changes have brought to light how little effect the Marxist-Leninist doctrines and their educational components have had on the minds of the majority of the adolescents in terms of those young persons' political and ideological commitment. However, the questions of how and to what extent this picture must be modified by inquiries into the deeper dimension of people's behaviors and attitudes is much more intricate; the questions cannot be dismissed by reference to the merely visible level of behavior and attitudes.

The postsocialist regimes in Eastern Europe sharply denounced the doctrinaire teaching structure that previously existed. Teachers had found themselves with the task of imparting those values that were legitimated by Marxist-Leninist ideology. Most of them, at the same time, were confronted with alternative or even contrasting value codes in their families, peer groups, religious communities, and other apolitical groups. In cases — and there were many — where teachers themselves were not committed to the official values they had to impart, the interpersonal conflict was reinforced by an inner, *intra*personal conflict. This conflict of public and private values resulted in the widespread existence of "schizophrenic" attitudes among teachers and, of course, among students, who, during their lessons, had to make statements that ran against their own convictions.

Now, after the revolutionary events of the past decade, it seems that adolescents can overcome the dissociation more easily than their teachers, including resolving their inner conflicts. And so we come back to Havel's argument that teachers' attitudes reflect those of the adult society as a whole. That means that even political dissent has not prevented people from internalizing certain basic — so called socialist — values and attitudes; and this has been criticized, though in highly exaggerated and even distorted form, by many West European commentators.

## The Basis for Current Issues and Trends

Multifarious approaches have arisen to innovation and reform in the education systems of Central and Eastern Europe. Most systems are still in a process of debate and initiation. The diversity, taken as a whole, can be traced back, first, to different national and regional traditions, as expressed in the deliberations of policymakers and educators. But they also mirror the scope of the revolutionary changes that have seized the political, social, and economic frameworks that are related to the education systems.

Because uncertainty is a significant factor at present, we must refrain from offering any definite analysis (Horváth and Mihály

1990; Krüger-Potratz 1990; Kuebart 1989; Mitter and Schaefer 1993). By constantly observing the scene, however, we may be able to draft some contours that indicate certain trends. With this limitation in mind, the following items should be understood as tentative, permitting — indeed encouraging — revisions and extensions.

1. The innovative approaches are focused on the *removal of all indoctrinating pressures* to which the socialist education systems were subjected by means of political power and ideological totalitarianism. It goes without saying that the opening toward a democratic and pluralistic self-awareness of education is highly dependent on political democratization. The state of the revolutionary process has become, for example, manifest in the closing down of university institutes and chairs that were devoted to one-sided investigation and transmission of Marxist-Leninist ideology or, when this was thought to be possible, in their transformation into institutes of sociological research. Other manifestations are the elimination of ideologically structured civics and the purification of curricula and syllabi in general and of susceptible subjects in particular, such as history and national literature (Nagy and Szebenyi 1990). Thus teachers have to tackle emergency situations in their everyday practice that are caused by the cancellation of certain syllabi and the withdrawal or selective use of hitherto "valid" textbooks. The latter procedure prevails in most cases because of the difficulties in quickly writing new textbooks and the obstacles to effective production. In many schools, old textbooks continue to be used with the offending pages or passages torn out or obliterated. All of these troubles affect the introduction of new regulations, especially with regard to examinations and, in particular, concerning secondary school terminal examinations and graduation examinations in higher education.

2. The attainment of intellectual freedom and plurality is closely connected to *a new way of handling the steering mechanism of the education system* and therefore to the role of the state in edu-

138

cation policy. We should not be surprised that, absent the former bureaucratic pressure on students, teachers, and parents to conform to ideology and the discipline of the approved hierarchy, calls for autonomy have been heard. The current discussions of how to implement autonomy within education policy and in the classroom are distinguished from similar discussions in Western Europe by the fierce tenacity of the proponents of autonomy.

A significant example is a development in Hungary. In 1985 the Hungarian parliament, still under the control of the socialist United Labor Party, enacted an Education Act that included features of reform. In particular, it confirmed the first steps toward decentralizing the network of responsibilities in the education system, which had been initiated already in the late 1970s. The act stressed the need for granting internal autonomy to schools as well as to individual teachers and students. The subsequent revolutionary changes in 1989 seemed to move this process forward, but now within the framework of democratic policies (Halász and Lukács 1990). However, financial problems and the neglect of national cohesion, supported by basic objections against a state withdrawal from education policy by the new political leaders, have caused a certain regression from the autonomy concept. Rather, the approach has become a middle-of-the-road solution, namely, the establishment of regional offices with control over the profession. These offices, directed by the Ministry of Education, also provide support for individual schools.

In general, one can observe in Eastern and Central Europe a certain (albeit varied) pulling back from certain forms of autonomy, such as from the election of head teachers (as practiced in Hungary and the former Soviet Union) and 50% representation by students in decision making at universities and other higher education offices (for example, in former Czechoslovakia). The recent changes signal disillusion with unfulfilled expectations and, moreover, call attention to arguments saying that autonomy has to be in congruence with the responsibility of the State in matters of nationwide requirements and needs. In retrospect, in recent developments in Central and Eastern Europe, it seems indeed that this issue often had been neglected in debates, legislative initiatives, and pilot projects (Anweiler 1990; Mitter 1990).

3. The Hungarian sociologist Tamas Kozma has identified the socialist society as an educationally affluent society (Kozma 1989). His thesis is worth mentioning in this connection because it points to one of the essential reasons for the inflexibility and rigidity of the education systems in the countries of the former socialist bloc. Concomitant with *the move from comprehensive planning by the State authorities to the re-establishment of the market and to the restitution of private property*, one has to study models and arguments for decoupling education and employment systems. Above all, this issue is particularly relevant because of the necessity to cut the ties between school-leaving certification and job guarantees. This reform must be made because many job guarantees even included advancement to certain rungs of the employment hierarchy (Halász and Lukács 1990).

However, the overall effect of this change must be gauged by observing its specific effect on upper secondary (general and vocational) and higher education admission policies. These changes confront policymakers in the areas of economy and education with tasks to which they are not accustomed (Kuebart 1990). Moreover, one has to consider the subjective side of these consequences, insofar as young people with secondary and higher education certificates care about finding jobs; and an available job need not coincide with one's former qualification. The issue of decoupling also has been discussed intensively in Western countries, particularly during the past 20 years. One must regard this issue as connected to traditional career paths, for example, from earning a teaching certificate and being appointed to a teaching position (Mitter 1978). However, such linkage occurred only in some sectors of employment, and even there it now has been long abandoned, for example, as in the (old) Federal Republic of Germany. Thus some natural changes have occurred in addition to the radical changes that took place at the end of the 1980s, when in some former socialist countries — Hungary is notable — the pendulum swung to the other side, opening job regulations to strict market-dominated norms (Kozma 1990).

High esteem for free-market philosophies has encouraged another sociopolitical trend that directly influences vocational and higher education policies. Having gotten rid of the tight budgetary and organizational fetters of socialist planning, advocates plead for including vocational and higher education in the rules of supply and demand; and their ideas are meeting with interest and acceptance. But overestimating the possible speed of such a radical change, particularly in systems with strict state-supervised management and financing, inevitably leads to disappointment and failure. The aforementioned development in Hungary — where radical decentralization of education management and free financing had been propagated at the end of the 1980s — exemplifies a situation in which it was necessary to return to more state responsibility. Such state direction, of course, need not result in the restoration of the former rigidities.

4. Considering the monopoly of uniform socialist schools during the past decades, one should not be surprised at hard debates concerning their future. Three central issues are being discussed. First, questions have been raised about the *length of compulsory schooling and its demarcation from the general and vocational education institutions at the upper secondary level*. In the majority of Central and Eastern European states the uniform school was stabilized as an 8-year school. Compulsory attendance was, as a rule, for 10 years, and thus extended into the upper secondary level by two grades. In Czechoslovakia the 8-year uniform school (introduced in 1976 and implemented during subsequent years) was extended to nine years in 1989, thereby reaching the condition that had existed before 1976.

In all Eastern European countries there have been extended debates about the introduction of 10-year uniform schools. However, this project was implemented only in the German Democratic Republic. An analogous concept in Poland (in 1973) was canceled in the beginning of the 1980s, mainly for financial reasons but also as a result of debates about the length of compulsory general education *per se* (von Kopp 1992; Kupisiewicz 1991; Mitter, Weiss, and Schaefer 1992).

Second, legal provisions and debates deal with *differentiation at the level of secondary education* according to student achievement and interests. In this respect two main variations can be noticed. The moderate variant, which predominates in legislative and administrative measures, concentrates on the maintenance of a school to be attended by *all* children and adolescents between ages 6 and 14 (15 or 16 in some cases). Such differentiation affects the development of options by reducing mandatory courses, which affects, in turn, the content of the core curriculum; and this is a source of controversy.

A more radical variation is the return to bipartite or tripartite systems and focused on the revival of the 8-year *Gymnasia*. Traditional schools of this sort have been restored in the form of alternative schools in Hungary and Czechoslovakia, mostly as a result of grassroots (frequently private) initiatives. In other Eastern European countries the reopening of such schools is still in a stage of debate.

The discussion of the third issue has already led to various pilot projects. This issue is the reduction of the overload of syllabi (Kozma 1987; Prucha 1989) and the *revision of instructional methods* to replace conventional forms of receptive learning and authoritarian teaching with open forms based on dialogue and communication, in close linkage with principles of education for democracy. It must be added that this debate already had been started in Central and Eastern Europe in the 1970s and 1980s, before *perestroika* and the revolutionary changes at the end of the 1980s. Reforms aimed at open forms of teaching and learning have to overcome traditional attitudes and expectations among teachers and administrators, as well as among parents, everywhere in the world, and so it goes without saying that attempts at generalizing pilot projects necessarily meet resistance in the postsocialist education systems (Razumovskij 1990; Sadrikov 1990).

5. *Vocational education* also has been involved in critical discussions. Here, however, the controversies do not affect the foundations of the achievement standard that, particularly in some of the Central European countries, enjoys a relatively high international reputation. This is true both of full-time technical schools (especially in Hungary, the Czech Republic, Slovakia, Slovenia, and Croatia) and dual training programs (in the same countries, part of the German and Austrian influence from the pre-World War II period).

Special attention also should be given to the diversified sector of technical secondary schools combining vocational qualification with the school-leaving certification of general secondary schooling, including the certificate holder's right to apply for entry to higher education. Such schools offering double qualification have achieved a higher reputation, especially among male adolescents. However, critical comments have been made regarding technological backwardness compared to modern standards in Western countries. Other criticism deals with the overspecialized structure of training courses. Observers have pointed out that many training courses cannot meet requirements for economic progress in a satisfactory way.

Finally, the opening of the employment system to the free market and privatization raises fundamental questions about the organization and finance of vocational education, which had been totally monopolized by the state. Recent observations, therefore, note regressive trends, particularly in dual training arrangements, resulting from the state's withdrawal from its responsibilities (Mitter, Weiss, and Schaefer 1992).

6. *Universities and polytechnics* also have been subjected to harsh criticism for their backward training programs and research capacities. Therefore, on the level of higher education, autonomy has become increasingly relevant and points the way to the return of academic self-governance in the form of the elected rectors, senators, deans, and other leading persons. Structural and curricular reforms are aimed, above all, at modernization. As far as orga-

nizational structures are concerned, efforts have been taken to overcome the rigid grading systems according to which, as in primary and secondary schools, students are promoted from one year to the next. Instead, open arrangements are proposed, and recommendations have been made to adjust the existing degree standards in order to make them conform with Western education standards demarcating undergraduate from graduate study.

Additionally, the universities emphasize the need to regain research as an essential component linked with teaching. The socialist regime allocated the bulk of research to academies or other extra-university research institutions or to firms. This policy was dictated by the demand to adjust the research capacities directly to the requirements of economic planning and contributed a good deal to the decline in quality at many universities (Kuebart 1990; Soljan 1991). Yet the new demand raises complex problems. First, the extra-university research institutions, in particular the academies of sciences, are not willing to see their capacities restricted or to share them with the universities. Therefore, they have started campaigns to prove the benefit of their contributions. Second, the universities are having tremendous internal troubles with their teaching obligations in a period of apparently increasing enrollments and so are hardly prepared to cope with the new challenge. Third, the universities lack scientists with research capacities, and they lack equipment. Finally, the reorganization of the national research system must be seen in connection with the reform of interrelations between research and the economy under free-market conditions.

7. *The revival of nationalism and ethnocentrism* throughout Eastern Europe has exercised great influence on organizational structures and curricula, from legal and administrative provisions down to individual schools and classrooms. This issue is too complex to be elaborated here. It will be sufficient to identify two essential curricular issues. The first is mother-tongue teaching and multilingual education, which have gained high relevance in education policies. The second is education for citizenship, primarily

144

institutionalized in the subject of civic education (Rajangu 1993; Yarmachenko 1992).

Solutions in most places are complicated by the fact that ethnic and linguistic demarcations rarely coincide with national (or regional) boundaries. Therefore civic education necessarily involves conflicts of expectations, goals, and contents wherever the norms and value systems of the state and the nondominant group(s) collide. This texture of conflicts has an immediate effect on the grassroots level of the school system, because it also affects attitudes of students and teachers. This problem also concerns the political cohesion of the state, which presupposes the loyalty of all it citizens, including those whose ethno-cultural loyalty is not congruent with that of the dominant group.

The preceding discussion has focused on basic issues. It should be completed by some considerations with regard to the overall state of affairs. First of all, two sectors of upper secondary education — the primary and the general — have not been given explicit attention. The reason is that these stages are comparatively consolidated. However, this observation should not lead to the erroneous assumption that the curricular and pedagogic concerns of this analysis are not relevant to these two stages. Likewise, I also must comment on preschool education, which enjoyed rather a good place in education policies. The recent austerity measures have seriously affected this stage of schooling because many kindergartens and other preschool institutions had been run by state-owned firms, whose collapse or privatization has resulted in their closing.

These issues and the larger issues enumerated previously are based on the idea of maintaining the state monopoly of responsibility for the education system. A counter-development is the effort in many quarters to establish private schools. We can observe a wide range of such alternatives. First, they concern the restoration or establishment of schools run by the big religious communities. In Poland and Hungary this sector has never disappeared from the scene, in spite of remarkable restrictions. In the rest of Central and Eastern Europe there have been entirely new initiatives.

Second, recent developments in the whole region, including the Russian Federation and other republics of the CIS, give evidence of the emergence of private initiatives (in the narrower sense), either aimed at the restoration of traditional schools or at the re-emergence of what is commonly called progressive education or the reform movement in education (*Reformpädagogik*). In this context special mention should be made about the Free Waldorf Schools, which have gained striking attractiveness in Hungary and Czechoslovakia. At this moment, it remains an open question whether this attractiveness of private education is only a symptom of radical reaction to the former rigid state monopoly and therefore perhaps a fashion, or if this trend will continue, thus paralleling the increased interest that private schools have gained in Western countries (Mitter 1990).

Summing up, the basic issues of present-day changes and trends must be considered as a fundamental challenge to the societies and to all people involved in education. They appeal, on one hand, to the wide range of non-formal educators, from the parents to the media. On the other hand, it is the teachers who have to cope with overcoming the socialist past in their day-to-day professional practice and who can be successful only on the basis of their personal engagement (Nagy and Szebenyi 1990; Pachocinski 1992; Phillips and Kaser 1992; Svecová 1992). Success or failure must depend on a socioeconomic framework that is far from satisfactory.

Moreover, the quality of education and teaching is rooted in the innovative resources of preservice and inservice teacher education. Legal documents bear witness to the importance of structural and curricular reforms focused on those open forms of teaching and learning that are required in the school practice. However, it does not seem for the time being that this task will be given the weight it needs. Thus the recent trends of teacher education in Eastern Europe show that involving teachers in most countries appears to be the weakest link in the chain of measures designed

146

to form plans and political declarations into legal regulations and daily practice.

Furthermore, the crisis concerning the teaching profession and teacher education is reinforced by two special components. First, providing trainees and teachers with qualities needed in Central and Eastern Europe requires qualified teacher trainees to be available in universities, colleges of education, and other training institutions. However, here we are reminded of the aforementioned confusions in which teachers are involved. Teaching in Central and Eastern Europe is predominantly a task for women. Their everyday overload, resulting from the difficulties in linking professional and private responsibilities under poor economic conditions, has not lessened with the collapse of the socialist regime; on the contrary, it has increased because of the challenges of the transformation process. This, of course, weakens motivation for innovative commitment. Second, women especially suffer from the dismissal measures that I referred to in my introduction to this essay.

## Between Retrospect and Prospect

The current debates that have seized the education systems in Central and Eastern Europe and the former Soviet Union are closely related to some retrospective and prospective considerations. The prospective orientations aim to attain the modern standards that are being discovered in Western countries, or thought to exist only there (Horváth and Mihály 1990). The introduction of information technology into the syllabi appears as a particularly relevant domain. In general, the search for efficiency and modernity is, as a rule, connected with looking out for examples in the West, whereby, among the competing targets, progressive and traditional education systems can be discerned.

It is not surprising that in such orientations prospective expectations and retrospective pictures overlap. For example, those who plead for emulating Sweden tend to focus their attention on the large-scale reforms of that country during the 1960s and 1970s without taking into adequate account the recent reconsiderations and actions and without special regard for cost factors during a period of austerity. Another example is the favorable view of the traditional *Gymnasia* of Germany. But proponents tend to neglect the considerable internal changes these schools have undergone during the past two decades, and they pay too little attention to the debates in Germany about the future of secondary education.

In higher education the Western models have displayed early attractiveness, not only in their internal structures but also regarding management and finance and the status of private universities. But the observer also can take notice of the revival of Wilhelm von Humboldt's university idea, which had a strong effect on universities in the whole of Central and Eastern Europe during the 19th century; and those ideas were not extinguished during the socialist period.

Westward orientation is reinforced by the recent changes in foreign language priority, namely, from Russian to Western languages (English in the first place, followed by German and French). In this context one should not overlook those reasonable arguments that contend that Russian should not be neglected among the neighbors of the CIS; at present they hardly receive the attention they should in that region. For the member countries of the CIS this question could attain vital importance, because abolishing or even confining the learning of Russian would deprive that region of its *lingua franca*.

All of the initiatives that have been taken in order to overcome former stagnation and backwardness are linked with efforts to find partners for cooperation in the West. One mainstream goes to North America, where many universities and research institutes (in Canada and the United States) have established extended scholarship programs for lecturers and students from Eastern Europe. Western Europe is the goal of the other mainstream. Here the European Community has taken initiatives in creating exchange programs between Western and Eastern European universities within a project called TEMPUS. TEMPUS I (1990-93) included programs between partners in the European Community (EC) and

Poland, Hungary, Czechoslovakia, Romania, Bulgaria, the Baltic States, Slovenia (replacing former Yugoslavia), and Albania. TEMPUS II (1994-98) envisages expanding to the CIS.

Vocational education is included in the PHARE program organized by the European Community Centre for the Development of Vocational Training (CEDEFOP) as a platform for meetings between East and West. So far, Hungary and Poland have been identified in the East European countries. Both of the EC projects are based on the conditions that Central and Eastern European institutions, as well as Western European institutions, must be engaged.

Beyond these supranational initiatives, attention should be paid to the increasing range of bilateral programs that are aimed at convening policymakers and administrators and at initiating exchange programs among schools and nonformal institutions, such as choirs, bands, and orchestras. Limitations on all these initiatives sometimes are caused by one-stream tendencies — for example, from East to West but not vice versa. International conferences organized by UNESCO and the Council of Europe are worth special attention, because they play a significant role in encouraging communication and interaction across the historical West-East border.

The efforts to overcome the socialist past are remarkably supported by recent events, and educators are actively involved in the people's desire for determining their sociocultural and political identities. These processes are complex and often confusing, insofar as they tend to be anchored to a democratic past that never existed — at least not in the sense it is perceived — with the exception of the former Czechoslovakia, which was the only genuine democracy in Central Europe during the interwar period (1918-38) (Phillips and Kaser 1992). Patriotism comes into the picture, too, albeit often distorted by nationalism, intolerance, and even war and genocide. It has a hold in all of the countries discussed in this essay, though to a higher or lower degree in the now-unraveled Yugoslavia and in parts of the former Soviet Union.

The significance of historical perspectives in the transformation process should not be underestimated as contributions to the reconstruction of identities. But such revivals are increasingly amalgamated with the creation of legends glorifying the nation's own past, while degrading that of neighbors and minorities. Russia deserves special attention again, with regard to the observation that during Perestroika a great number of Russian educators began by looking back to what they considered to be their great past in the "Golden Twenties" (Razumovskij 1990). Increasingly, however, investigations and reflections pass the Rubicon of the October Revolution and include Russia's history of education in the 19th century and the beginning of the 20th century, which is rich indeed in educational and pedagogic models.

## Concluding Remarks

Current developments in the education systems of the former socialist countries, with their various approaches to reform and innovation, do not yet allow any definite predictions. At this moment the whole region is involved in transitional processes, whereby education must be seen in close relation with the overarching socioeconomic, cultural, and political transformation process (Gershunskij 1992).

Remembering the enormous troubles on the economic scene, one can conclude that the march into the future is more than gloomy. The internal attitude problems in all of the Eastern European countries aggravate the crisis probably even more than economic and financial austerity. Special consideration must be given to the dissolution of the Soviet Union, the collapse of Yugoslavia, and, though with much lower apprehensions, the dissolution of the Czechoslovak Federal Republic. Moreover, each of these countries has to cope with multinationality issues resulting from their prerevolutionary inheritance and from the problematic Soviet migration policies, the results of which can be seen in the current internal disarray in the liberated Baltic States.

Apart from the troubles caused by the economic, political, and sociocultural crisis, schools must overcome enormous internal difficulties. They must cope with structural stagnation and curricular content that has become obsolete. Democratization and autonomy can be identified as basic concerns indeed. Yet illusory expectations must give way to realistic appraisals that show that many problems can be solved only by continuous efforts. The warnings against hasty and unconsidered borrowing of Western examples have gained great relevance. They concern the overestimation of certain structural and curricular achievements of Western education systems; frequently the Eastern counterparts do not give special attention to the conditions under which those examples exist. In particular, such borrowing neglects the long and hard experiences of Western education *before* such achievements were reached — and the fact that such achievements also need much fine-tuning in the West.

In the relation between the education system and the labor market, the socialist experiences — though based on the principle of merging training, research, and production — are unlikely to be helpful for developing future-oriented models. These must follow the idea of free partnership between education institutions (in particular on the vocational and higher levels) and firms, whereby transitional solutions are inevitable, again to be contrasted with short-term free-market euphoria.

Whether education is able to take its necessary role in the progress of the Central and Eastern European states will depend on how and to what extent a balance between initiatives, continuous efforts, and realistic expectations can be achieved and maintained. In addition, Western expertise and advice is needed on all levels. Exchanges of teachers, students, administrators, and managers offer significant support for innovative efforts; probably they are more important than material help. Stating this does not mean, of course, neglecting the need to provide education establishments in Eastern Europe with modern equipment and means of improving information, teaching, and learning.

The collapse of the socialist regimes in Eastern Europe has broadened and intensified the foundations for the universal development of education to be built on international and intercultural communication, understanding, and tolerance. However, this challenge can be met only if *all* the internal and international obstacles are identified and removed. Education for democracy must be considered as a focal point in this overarching context.

## References

Anweiler, O. "Politischer Umbruch und Pädagogik im östlichen Europa." *Bildung und Erziehung* 43 (1990): 237-47.

Anweiler, O., ed. *Systemwandel im Bildungs- und Erziehungswesen in Mittel- und Osteuropa.* Berlin: Arno Spitz, 1992.

Bachmeier, P., ed. *Bildungspolitik in Osteuropa: Systemwandel und Perspektiven.* Wien: Jugend und Volk, 1991.

Baske, S. "Charakteristika der Entwicklung und der gegenwärtigen Gestalt des Bildungswesens in Mitteleuropa im inter- und intrasystemaren Vergleich." *Zeitschrift für Ostforschung* 39 (1990): 226-37. a

Baske, S. "Perestrojka als Aufgabe der Bildungspolitik." In *Multidisziplinäre Veröffentlichung*, vol. 1. Berlin: Osteuropa-Institut an der Freien Universität Berlin, 1990. b

Baske, S. "Der Übergang von der marxistisch-leninistischen zur freiheitlich-demokratischen Bildungspolitik in Polen." *Osteuropa* 40 (1990): 966-74. c

Báthory, Z. "Decentralisation Issues in the Introduction of the New Curriculum: The Case of Hungary." *Prospects* 16 (1990): 34-47.

Davydov, V.V., and Nikandrov, N.D. "Bildung und Erziehung in der Sowjetunion in den neunziger Jahren." *Bildung und Erziehung* 44 (1991): 167-75.

Dienys, V. "Education Reform in Lithuania: Main Trends and Problems." Policy report. Strasbourg: Council of Europe, 1992.

Dunstan, J., ed. *Soviet Education Under Perestroika.* New York: Routledge, 1992.

Gershunskij, B.S. "Russia: Education and the Future." Unpublished paper. Moscow: Russian Academy of Education, 1992.

Gershunskij, B.S., and Pullin, R.T. "Current Dilemmas for Soviet Secondary Education: An Anglo-Soviet Analysis." *Comparative Education* 26 (1990): 307-18.

Górnikowska-Zwolak, E., and Radziewicz-Winnicki, A. *Educational and Social Transformation in Poland and Other Post-Communist Countries.* Katowice, Poland: LW-Press, 1992.

Halász, G., and Lukács, P. *Educational Policy for the Nineties: Theses for a New Concept of State Educational Policy.* Budapest: Hungarian Institute for Educational Research, 1990.

Havel, V. *Sommermeditationen*. Translated from the Czech by J. Bruss. Berlin: Rowohlt, 1992.

Horváth, A., and Mihály, O. "Globalization of Education and Eastern Europe." *Prospects* 20 (1990): 145-54.

von Kopp, B. "The Eastern European Revolution and Education in Czechoslovakia." *Comparative Review of Education* 36 (1992) 101-13.

Kozakiewicz, M. "Educational Transformation Initiated by the Polish Perestroika." *Comparative Review of Education* 36 (1992): 91-100.

Kozma, T. "Common Cores in the Primary Curricula: Some Experiments in European Socialist Education." *Zeitschrift für internationale erziehungs- und sozialwissenschaftliche Forschung* (1987): 101-24.

Kozma, T. "An Educationally Affluent Society? Key Issues in Hungarian Educational Policy." *Perspectives in Education* 5 (1989): 223-32.

Kozma, T. "Education in Eastern Europe: The New Conservative Wave." *Anthropology of East European Review* 9 (1990): 18-30.

Krüger-Potratz, M. "Vergleichende Erziehungswissenschaft und pädagogische Osteuropaforschung. Im Lichte der Umbrüche in den Gesellschaften sowjetischen Typs." *Osteuropa* 40 (1990): 935-46.

Kuebart, F. "Soviet Education and Comparative Research: A German View." *Comparative Education* 25 (1989): 283-92.

Kuebart, F. "Kader für die Perestrojka. Zu Konzeption und Verlauf der sowjetischen Hochschulreform." *Osteuropa* 40 (1990): 947-62.

Kupisiewicz, C. "Die Expertenberichte von 1973 und 1989 zum Stand des Bildungswesens in Polen-Entstehung, Inhalt und Funktion." *Bildung und Erziehung* 44 (1991): 39-52.

Mitter, W. *Secondary School Graduation: University Entrance Qualification in Socialist Countries. A Comparative Study*. Oxford: Pergamon Press, 1978.

Mitter, W. "Das Bildungswesen in Osteuropa im Umbruch. Rückblick und Ausblick in historisch-vergleichender Sicht." *Osteuropa* 40 (1990) 909-24.

Mitter, W.; Weiss, M.; and Schaefer, U., eds. *Recent Trends in East European Education*. Frankfurt am Main: German Institute for International Educational Research, 1992.

Mitter, W., and Schaefer, U., eds. *Upheaval and Change in Education*. Frankfurt am Main: German Institute for International Educational Research, 1993.

Muckle, J. *Portrait of a Soviet School Under Glasnost*. Basingstoke: MacMillan, 1990.

Nagy, M. "Survey Study into Conditions, Problems and Policy of Education in Central Europe: The Case of Hungary." Policy report. Amsterdam: Network Educational Science, 1992.

153

Nagy, M., and Szebenyi, P. *Curriculum Policy in Hungary*. Budapest: Hungarian Institute for Educational Research, 1990.

Pachocinski, R. "Survey Study into Conditions, Problems and Policy of Education in Central Europe: The Case of Poland." Unpublished paper. Amsterdam: Network Educational Science, 1992.

Phillips, D., and Kaser, M., eds. *Education and Economic Change in Eastern Europe and the Former Soviet Union*. Wallingford: Triangle Books, 1992.

Prucha, J. "Educational Reform in Socialist Countries." Paper presented at the Conference on "Education in Europe: The Challenge of 1992" sponsored by Professors World Peace Academy, Budapest, 20-24 October 1989.

Prucha, J. "Education in Transition: The Czech Republic." Unpublished paper. Prague: Institute of Educational and Psychological Research, 1992.

Prucha, J., and Walterova, E. *Education in a Changing Society: Czechoslovakia*. Prague: Nakladatelsté a vydavatelstvi H+H, 1992.

Rajangu, V. *Das Bildungswesen in Estland*. Köln and Wien: Böhlau Verlag, 1993.

Razumovskij, V.G. "Inhalte der mittleren Bildung in der UdSSR." *Bildung und Erziehung* 43 (1990): 159-76.

Sadrikov, V.D. "Neue Pädagogik oder die Pädagogik der Freiheit." *Bildung und Erziehung* 43 (1990): 292-311.

Soljan, N.N. "The Saga of Higher Education in Yugoslavia." *Comparative Education Review* 35 (1991): 131-53.

Strajn, D. *Slovenia: Democracy as a Quality of Education*. Strasbourg: Council of Europe, 1992.

Svecová, J. "Survey Study into Conditions, Problems and Policy of Education in Central Europe: The Case of Czechoslovakia." Unpublished paper. Amsterdam: Network Educational Science, 1992.

Yarmachenko, N. "Functions of General Secondary Education in the Formation of World Outlook." Unpublished paper. Strasbourg: Council of Europe, 1992.

# Education for Democracy in Russia

## BY ABDUSALAM GUSSEINOV
(translated by R.G. Apressyan)

My intention in this essay is to present a general outline of changes that have taken place in the Russian system of education. I shall consider the following issues: 1) the Soviet system of education, its character, and the causes of its crisis; 2) democratic reforms in Russian education; 3) the new model of teaching humanities and social-political science; and 4) education and upbringing.

### The Soviet System of Education: Character and Crisis

The idea of education is fundamentally united with the idea of personal freedom and democracy in the Western European philosophical tradition and sociocultural experience. The Western way of thinking follows a belief that knowledge and the culture of reason secure the competence and responsibility for actions. That is why an educated and competent person is thought to be a mature, self-dependent person, who does not need paternalist surveillance (especially on the part of the state) and who can see and does not need a guide. Ignorance is a sort of blindness; an educated person is like one who can see. In the Western tradition, education is a means to the intellectual and spiritual emancipation of a human being. That is why it necessarily must be general, and that general education has been one of the most prominent features of democracy in its modern sense.

In the Russian historical context, the idea of education has undergone essential changes. Knowledge was considered 1) as a

155

means to the effective functioning of the state, rather than for the upbringing of a personality, and 2) as an obligation of the privileged classes. Education in Russia was like state conscription, which mainly burdened the nobility. In particular, Russian history does not have the phenomenon of the free, autonomous university, though some professors and academics were pressing for it. Russian universities, as well as the Russian Academy of Sciences, were imperial. The well-known Russian historian, V.O. Kliutchevsky, characterized in 1908 the official approach toward education since the middle of 17th century:

> Public education has become like a governmental target for the state delivery of youths for training according to a definite program: Military schools for noble juveniles, schools of engineering, societies for the education of noble and bourgeois young girls, academies of arts, and gymnasiums were established. Tropical plants were grown in lordly greenhouses. However no real people's schools of general education, or agricultural schools, had been established during two centuries. . . . The state was implanting in the society a roughly pragmatic view of science as a means for advancement and bribes. At the same time it was forming a new serving caste from the high classes, mainly from the nobility. This serving caste was separated from the people by privileges and class prejudices, but even more by official abuses. (*Works*, vol. 3, p. 11)

The Soviet regime took a dual approach toward the traditional Russian education policy. It was characterized by the termination of some practices and the succession of others. Like the tzars, the Soviet regime continued to consider education in terms of state interests, though it drastically rejected class education for general education. The Soviet system of education arose as a convergence of two ideas: the Russian idea of a national destiny for education and the European idea of general education. Two radical points might be especially stressed: The tzar's power ultimately could not subordinate education to the state, and the Western democracies could not consistently realize the principle of general education and its equal accessibility to all citizens, which education under the Soviets had succeeded in doing.

Although the Soviet system of education, like the entire Soviet governance system, has become the property of history, the time for its comprehensive analysis and evaluation has not yet come. That will be possible only on the basis of a new system that replaces the former one. Society in transition is tricky ground for historical observations. What the society is getting rid of is clear, but it is not clear where that society is going. A transitional period usually excites emotions and replaces rational analysis with declarations of desires. As a result, the future seems to be majestic and close to the present, and the past insignificant and distant. That is why I shall briefly characterize the principles of the Soviet system of education and its results and then outline the ongoing reforms in the Russian system of education.

The Soviet system of education was a peculiar phenomenon, its nature not yet completely understood. It was characterized by several factors:

1. *The cult of knowledge* based on the ideal of scientific determinism. One could find Francis Bacon's statement, "Knowledge is power," as a poster in almost all Soviet schools. All the problems of human life were considered to have their best solutions only within this framework. Therefore it was considered best to have as much knowledge as was available. A person whose head was loaded with diverse and systematized knowledge was a typical product of the Soviet system of education.

2. *Social pragmatism.* Scientific knowledge is diverse. The variety of subjects is reflected in the variety of professions, and the Soviet system of education was targeted to provide for all existing professions. Secondary schools gave pupils the basics in the sciences in order to prepare them for probable further specialization. Technical schools and higher education prepared and trained students directly according to the requirements of different branches of the national economy. However, specialization focuses knowledge; it does not merely limit it. Although Soviet higher education was intended to coordinate specialization with encyclopedic

learning, the tasks of general education were dominated by pragmatic goals. Almost all of the graduating students (and half of them were engineers) were to be assigned by the state. Thus the system of education was an integral part of the planned economy.

3. *Limited freedom of personal choice.* The European ideal of enlightenment consists of two ideas: the cult of knowledge and the idea of free personality. The Soviet system cut down this ideal. While an adherent of the cult of knowledge, it was alien or even hostile to the idea of freedom. All the roles within it — a student, a teacher/professor, an official — were strictly determined. No room for freedom in individual activity was left. Pupils and students had no right to choose what to study or whose classes to attend. They were required to learn and master only what they were taught. There were no elective courses in secondary school, and there were almost no elective courses in colleges and universities. The system of education left for the student only the decision of what particular school to attend. Teachers, including university professors, also were limited in their activity. They were to function as transmitters of knowledge and were strongly obliged to follow the unified curricula. An official had the role of managing, but his main function was keeping vigilant watch over students and professors to see that they adhered to the given order. So there was an evident lack of what is called "academic freedom" in the Soviet system of education.

4. *Ideological dogmatism.* The system was closed and basically incapable of critical self-reflection. Its purposes and intentions were justified by the Marxist ideology that really was the state religion. It is significant that this ideology declared itself a science. The problem of the goals of education was solved very simply: One was to study to become useful to the people for the construction of communist society.

Every pupil or student knew Lenin's words: "Only by mastering the whole knowledge collected by mankind can one become a communist." But the question, *Why is it obligatory to become a communist?* was considered to be beyond discussion, if not absurd, like a question about the reasons to live. In the second half

158

of the 1950s, when I was a student in Moscow's Lomonosov University, we were shocked by the sudden news that one among us believed in God and was visiting a church. An earthquake or a Martian's appearance would hardly have surprised us as much as this news. Actually, this fact signified that somebody was hesitating about the communist ideal.

The problem of individual goals of education and motivation toward them was solved by the premise that scientific achievements belonged to the people. It was assumed that all working people had a desire for education. If some did not have a desire to study, they would be considered not to understand their own real good, and so they should be constrained to study. Society had diverse methods for such coercion. For instance, in the 1950s and early 1960s, especially in small towns, a father could be deprived of his over-fulfillment bonus or be materially punished in some other way if his son was not good in school.

5. *Recognition of the potential endowments of all students.* Soviet curricula, both at the school and the university levels, always were characterized by a comprehensive inclusiveness. The volume of information, as a rule, was beyond the students' abilities to learn. This fact, while perhaps irreproachable from a logical point of view, was vulnerable from the point of view of educational psychology. Every teacher faced a hard problem: To whom should the teacher orient instruction — to the good students, to the laggards, or to the undistinguished students?

The Soviet curricula were unconditionally aimed at the strongest students. They set a standard for learning that treated all students as if they were highly gifted. I remember that at the Faculty of Philosophy of the Moscow Lomonosov University we were recommended to read an amount of literature that we would fail to read even if we had been reading all day long. One might consider such a situation to be absurd. However, the paradox is that the evidently excessive curricular requirements, aiming the students at a very high or even unachievable maximum, were not frustrating students as one might expect. Just the contrary, they were creating an atmosphere of intellectual intensity and industry.

As a result, the pedagogical efforts were sufficiently successful. It is probably natural that results are as high as goals are harder.

Such were the general principles of the Soviet system of education. It was both a part of the Soviet state system and its means of perpetuation. Stalin once said about the Russian tsar-reformer Peter the Great that he eradicated barbarism by barbarous methods. Most likely, these words describe Stalin himself and Bolsheviks in general. In any case, these words characterized the Soviet system of education. It was a well-adjusted conveyor for the distribution of knowledge and for training the specialists required by the state.

I shall refrain from appraising this system, particularly in moral terms. However, anyone intending to make such an appraisal should take into consideration two important historical facts. First, within this system of education a half-educated Russia in a short time was transformed into a highly educated country — at the beginning of this century not more than 20% of Russians had even a primary education. Second, in many respects owing to this system of education, Russia gained extraordinary success in science and technology. One need only to consider, for example, its achievements in military technology or space development.

This Soviet system that arose during the 1930s came to a crisis in the 1960s. The crisis was determined by different causes. First — and this was common for the whole post-World War II European-American mentality — the ideal of scientific rationality and the belief in the power of reason began to be distrusted. Second, Soviets of new generations in the late 1950s and 1960s began more and more to orient themselves toward individual values. Third, the system of education became so broad and divergent that it was hard for the Communist Party and the state ideological institutions to manage and keep watch over it. Fourth, it appeared that the conveyor-like system of education that was developed from classical paradigms of determinism was difficult to adapt to the transmission of modern knowledge. It is a special research task to follow the effect of all these causes; thus I will describe only some signs of the crisis and signs of the society's attempts to overcome it.

The first public discussion that contained criticisms of the technocratic orientation in education started in the late 1950s and early 1960s. It was called a dispute of "physicists" and "lyricists" and dealt with the question whether a physicist should know and understand lyric poetry. The question was about the narrow-mindedness of the natural-scientific way of thinking and the necessity to supplement it with an aesthetic outlook.

Another discussion was devoted to academic rights, specifically to voluntary attendance at classes in universities. However, the hidden topic was about the freedom of students to miss the classes in Marxism-Leninism. This latent criticism of the ideological programming of education increased and sharpened with time. The official attempts to renovate humanitarian and political education by incorporating new courses, such as "basic social sciences" in secondary schools and "scientific communism" in higher education, had no positive results.

At the end of 1960s it appeared that the proportions of students from families of workers and peasants was rapidly diminishing. To stop this process, the state made some energetic efforts, for example, establishing special one-year courses designed to prepare workers' and peasants' children for colleges and universities. However, these attempts were countered by a general decrease in the level of education. Finally, at the end of the 1980s, it became evident that the Soviet system of education missed the computer stage of the scientific-technological revolution. This was the final sentence for the system.

Various attempts at universal reform of the Soviet system of education have been carried out during the last 35 years. The school terms were made shorter or longer. The curricula were changed, sometimes very seriously. Educators tried to bring the schools closer to life and to make pupils and students more interested in learning. However, the attempts were all in vain. It became evident that all the attempts to reform the system had actually failed, that the system itself should be changed. In fact, radical changes started after August 1991.

## Democratic Reforms in Russian Education

Three tendencies characterize the recent system of education in Russia: 1) democratization, 2) a material and financial slump, and 3) the loss of prestige of higher education and education in general. I shall attempt to portray these tendencies with regard to higher education.

I understand democratization in education as those changes in management, philosophy, and content of education that orient it toward liberal values. Already the state has no monopoly in education. Teaching institutions may be established by nongovernment entities, including foreign citizens. Today 140 non-state budget institutions of higher education of different kinds have been established. Sixty-seven of these have received licenses to issue certificates. These 67 educational institutions make up 10% of the nation's colleges and universities and prepare 4% of the students. Concurrently, the state higher education institutions have changed their status by becoming autonomous. However, national ruling bodies still influence education policy through finances and legislation.

Training specialists is no longer the only purpose of higher education. It now is oriented to satisfying the learning needs of individuals. Since March 1992 a multi-level system of higher education has been accepted: baccalaureate, master's, doctorate (*aspirantura*), and post-doctorate (*habilitation*). Education at each level is relatively autonomous and is completed by getting a certain degree. On the level of the baccalaureate a student can get a bachelor's degree or a certificate of incomplete education. On the level of the master's a student also has a double option: to get either a master's degree or a qualification certificate. Such a system promotes academic mobility and accepts a variety of motives for learning. Thus education becomes a sphere of individual development, rather than a starting condition of a social career.

Perhaps the most substantial change in education is that it is becoming ideologically unchained. According to state regulation, it is prohibited to establish organizational structures of political and religious movements in state and municipal education institutions. Universities and colleges independently determine their staff and curricula. In 1992 the Russian parliament accepted the Education Act, which secures the democratic reforms in this sphere. Such principles as freedom and pluralism in education, the humanitarian character of education, the priority of universal values, free individual development, the autonomy of educational institution, and the public and secular character of education are asserted in this act.

The material and financial conditions of secondary schools and higher education have been steadily decreasing in the last few years. Higher education receives only a quarter of the required budget allocation. According to the Education Act, a professor's salary must be twice as high as the average comparable salary in industry. However, in fact it is lower by almost half. Many young teachers leave the universities. Thus in Moscow alone about 3,000 teachers and professors have left, and many of those who have stayed are compelled to seek additional income. There are no finances for equipment, laboratories, libraries, or, in particular, for purchasing foreign literature. Classroom and dormitory buildings are in bad condition. Many are facing decay and destitution.

The prestige of higher education in Russia has fallen very low today. The absolute quantity of students has been decreasing over the past 10 years, with the ratio of students per 10,000 of population dropping to 14%. In the last few years the competition for entering even the "elite" education institutions has fallen.

Young people now tend to join the many businesses that are springing up and that promise quick and easy income. They realize that a social career today depends least of all on education, that specialized knowledge is in less demand because of financial and economic difficulties in high-tech industries and anarchy in state social policy. For example, last summer only 7 of 105 graduating students of the Moscow Physical-Technological Institute (the most prestigious school of its type) took jobs in their profession. In the opinion of the public, new, pragmatic, energetic, and lucky adventurers are increasing faster than are new, professionally educated people.

The worst feature is that these trends and the loss of prestige have coincided with democratic changes in higher education. Hence it is too easy to assume that democratization is a cause of these difficulties and that the public will associate these problems with democratization and will consider the problems as the price of freedom in this sphere.

## A New Model of Teaching Humanities and Social-Political Sciences

The essence of the changes in the Russian system of education may be described as a shift from the ideal of state destiny to the ideal of free personality. The success of the reforms largely depends on the changes in curricula, principally on humanitarian teaching of social-political subjects.

The old model of teaching social sciences was very simple. Teaching these subjects according to unified curricula and textbooks was obligatory in all higher education institutions. The curricula and textbooks were prepared mainly in Moscow, and the academic councils of institutions were not allowed to interfere with the curricula and their contents. The teaching process was watched by the Communist Party organization. This model was based, we can say, on the presumption of truth concerning society and humanity to be found in Marxist theory. The words "Marxism teaches" (or even "CPSU teaches") in the Soviet vocabulary meant much the same as "God said" in the vocabulary of a believer. Soviet ideological and political bodies were responsible for the isolation of social science education in that country from the civilized world and from Russian history. Thus in this sphere we need to speak about completely new tasks rather than merely renovating past practices and experience. At present, Russian higher education has started to accept and implement a new model of humanitarian and social-political education that is oriented toward the idea of dialogue between cultures and philosophies.

The fact is that under the present anarchy (which many people interpret as democracy), certain technical institutes have decided to reject some, if not most, subjects in the humanities and social sciences. That is why a list of obligatory subjects in the humanities and social sciences, for the baccalaureate level, has been announced by the federal commission for higher education. The list includes history, philosophy, the theory and history of culture, sociology, economics, political science, basic jurisprudence, psychology and pedagogy, and foreign languages. Some of these subjects must be taken by all students; others are elective. However, 25% (1,804 academic hours) of total class time must be devoted to these subjects. This step was the first of its kind.

The next step is to work out general standards of knowledge that will offer a general description of the basic content of courses adequate for the up-to-date treatment of a discipline. The standards differ from the obligatory curricula of the past in that they are not doctrinaire and do not require particular subjects in which this or that specific knowledge must be taught. For example, one of the nine articles of the state standards for philosophy includes such topics as human beings in the universe and religious, philosophical, and scientific pictures of the world.

Central control over these matters is determined by the necessity to create academic mobility and to "convert" specialists either within Russia or within the world community. Besides, such centralization secures a better quality of education.

However, an important problem is teaching personal. There now are almost 20,000 social science teachers in higher education in Russia, 9,000 of whom are specialists in subjects that no longer exist, such as the history of the Communist Party, scientific communism, and the party and Soviet state development. These teachers must either leave their positions or pass requalification courses. Others also require inservice training. The state policy is to give each teacher an opportunity to find himself or herself a new situation. For these purposes the Federal Committee (ministry) for Higher Education established a Center for Humanities Education with divisions of history, philosophy, economics, political science, and sociology. Mainly scholars from the Academy of Sciences and foreign scholars have been recruited into this project.

Moreover, the existing centers for inservice university teacher training, particularly in St. Petersburg and Ekaterinburg (in Soviet times, Sverdlovsk), have been rearranged. A separate project has been devoted to young teachers in the humanities and social sciences that proposes a series of summer schools and also sabbaticals in Western universities for the best young scholars.

Another activity concerns methodology in teaching the humanities and social and political science. To create new textbooks and readings, the federal committee for higher education, jointly with the Soros Foundation, arranged a competition called "Humanities Education in Higher Schools." More than 700 applications were received for the first round, and 184 of them were recommended for the second round. In addition, a certain number of foreign books and anthologies will be published.

It is evident that this task is not for one day. However, the main direction of these changes is clear: from ideologically oriented political education to humanitarian education based on liberal and democratic values, from political intolerance to dialogue, from social pragmatism to the ethics of personal responsibility.

## General Education and Moral Education.

The Soviet school was an institution for both general education and moral education. It was responsible both for the level of knowledge and competence of the younger generation and for that generation's spirit, mentality, and value orientations. The main task of the Soviet school from the primary level to the highest level was to bring up children and youngsters in a spirit of adherence to communist ideals and the socialist order. Moral education was interpreted as communist training. Lenin put forward its basic program in his 1920 speech, "The Tasks of Youth Leaders." The Communist Party constantly was specifying its particular tasks. Communist education was pursued by different methods and forms, specifically in activities of *Pioneers* (communist scouts) and *Comsomol* (young communists) organizations and, as they were called, "out of classroom" activities.

In present day Russia both the tasks of communist moral education and the corresponding pedagogical methods have been thrown out.* However, this does not mean that the schools have gotten rid of moral education. That would be impossible if only because a teacher is much more to a student than just a competent person in a particular subject. But morally neutral education would be purposeless as well, because knowledge can be used for both good and evil reasons. Aristotle pointed to the lack of coincidence of the intellectual and moral abilities of a human being. That is why, in addition to providing young people with knowledge, it is important to teach them how to use it.

The Russian school currently is challenged by the task of changing the nature of its role in providing moral education, specifically the goals and methods of moral education. This will become possible while Russian society itself is overcoming the spiritual chaos it now is experiencing, attaining a degree of stability of values, and finding a consensus among different social groups concerning the fundamental principles of its existence. For example, the problem of the language of communication appeared in the Soviet Union, which had been known as a multinational state, on the eve of its decay. This problem, though not in as sharp a form, remains a problem in post-Soviet Russia. However, the social-linguistic problem is secondary to the social-cultural problem. Because people in Russia lost a general sense of unity, they ceased to understand, see, and hear each other. They found themselves in different value spaces. Lacking common values, many Russians find that no social communication is possible. The main problem now is to elaborate a new universal *value language* for the society. Unlike the language of socialist ideology, this new language would provide an opportunity for dialogue between people of different social-political, religious, and other interests.

*This process began in the Brezhnev years, when everything that used to be called "communist upbringing" was made vapid. Its history in the Yeltsin counter-revolution consisted in the purposeful eradication of communism from the schools, often using schools for a no-less-purposeful spreading of anti-communism. This process itself is an interesting and instructive phenomenon.

Whatever particular expression it has, basically it must be the language of universal morality.

Taking this perspective into consideration, in conclusion I shall consider some theoretical issues of moral education. In its general scope, moral education can be described as a directed influence by some persons toward others for the purpose of teaching the latter certain ideas and actions that the former consider to be moral. This is one of the methods of moral inheritance in a society. In the history of culture there are at least four main traditions regarding the understanding of moral education: paternalist (directed to respecting elders); religious-clerical (directed to obedience to God), enlightenment (directed to knowledge and wherein reason is the judge); and communitarian (directed to communal values). These traditions were embodied — albeit inconsistently — in various conceptions. Their philosophical content is revealed in their answers to the fundamental question of the possibility of moral upbringing and its direction. While some conceptions suggested particular agendas for moral upbringing (as in the cases of Plato and Rousseau), they appeared to be utopian. These moralists and others proposed detailed, though unfeasible, projects that were like that jovial fraud who responded to criticism of his anti-mice powder by saying that the powder should have been put exactly into the mouse's mouth.

General conceptions of moral education cannot be converted into a particular chain of rationally arranged pedagogical procedures for achieving a proposed moral result. This is a crucial argument against such conceptions. Moreover, I have doubts concerning the intelligibility of the very term "moral education." All attempts to understand moral education as a particular kind of education, like aesthetic education or physical training, that is, as a special sphere of professional activity, lead to difficult controversies.

Moral education presupposes *educators*, that is, people competent in the appropriate spheres. It is consistent to assume that moral educators are individuals distinguished by their moral qualities. However, one of the essential features of a morally good person is a sense of self-discontent in his or her personal imperfection, owing to which he or she cannot take on the role of a teacher of morality. People's belief in their capability of playing the role of moral educator only proves their inadequacy for moral education. A paradox follows from this: One who has the qualities and skills necessary to become a teacher of morality will never become one, just because of having such qualities. Concomitantly, we should not trust a person who desires to become a teacher of morality, specifically because of this desire.

There also are controversies concerning the objective of moral education. Education is based on a division of people into those who teach and those who are taught. But morality cannot be mastered externally. The idea of personal autonomy is fundamental to morality; hence the moral law, unlike all other laws, arises from within a person. Usually this controversy is resolved by understanding moral education as the art of midwifery, as expressed, for example, by Socrates and Kant.

Education, like any rational activity, presupposes a distinction between the result (the goal) and the acts leading to it (the means), under which the acts-means get their sense and justification in relation to the given goal. (To become good at hammering one needs to pass a period of training, and at the beginning a hammer very often hits one's fingers; to become good at playing the piano one has to endure long periods of daily exercises.) However, the achievement of the goals of education find justification in a broader scope of life, that is, a means to a more important and higher goal. Thus mastering practical or artistic skills is directly related to the material welfare of an individual, to his or her social self-image and status.

Moral education is beyond the logic of rational, expedient activity. Moral goodness is not an ordinary goal that can be gained in a definite period of time by certain actions. More plausibly, moral goodness can be called the ultimate or highest goal, which gives rise to all other goals and is located at the foundation, rather than at the top, of human activity. More correctly, it is not a goal, but an ideal — the regulative principle and criterion of human conduct. The formula, *The end justifies the means*, is not part of morality.

There are no means that lead to morality. Morality also cannot become a means leading to something else, for virtue is the only reward for virtue.

There is another controversy: Moral education as a rationally organized activity could be intelligible in so far as morality, as an ideal, was transformed by this activity into a real goal. However, if morality is an ideal, all efforts to transform it are senseless, for it cannot lose its existence as an ideal without losing its existence altogether.

The fact of the absence of persons and institutions professionally engaged in moral education and responsible for it is important for understanding the social reproduction of morality. Plato, in *Protagorus*, described the debate between Protagorus and Socrates concerning the possibility of teaching people morality. Like other sophists, Protagorus gave a positive answer to this question. Socrates asked why, in that case, ethical people had not taught their children the same and why there were no special teachers of virtue, as there are teachers of music, gymnastics, or mathematics. Arguing cogently and admirably, Protagorus maintained that there were no teachers in morality and there was no real need for such teachers, because all other teachers (of music, gymnastics, or mathematics) were actually teachers of morality as well. All the social institutions (family, school, constitution, and so on), besides their direct goals, also have a moral influence on people.

The social reproduction of morality is incorporated in the variety of social activities and is realized along the way. In general, it is spontaneous. One can manage and control it through self-education and self-perfection. Nobody has a special privilege to speak on behalf of morality and to represent the public interests in this sphere. Everyone possesses this privilege and can be committed to it. As a social, active, and rational being, a person is fully responsible for his or her own moral upbringing and development.

Human beings can purposefully direct their own moral development by certain conduct, which in turn creates corresponding personal qualities or states of character. As Aristotle said, the moral principles of the society are like the actions that flow from them. Equally distributing goods among people, a person becomes just; accustoming oneself to face danger with courage, a person becomes courageous. And, through one's deeds, one can morally influence others. "Moral education starts when people stop using words," commented Albert Schweitzer. That is, it achieves its goal by the power of one's personal patterns of action and not by preaching. In this way, action is the basis for moral self-education and for moral influence on others. Thus a student becomes an educator; and by educating oneself, a person teaches others.

Hence moral education is impossible as an institutional and strictly regulated process. Once someone undertakes to institutionalize moral education, as a rule it assumes perverted forms, specifically such extremes as moralizing or moral terror. Moralizing overestimates personal good will, replaces practical problems by hypothetical moral ones, and confuses their solution with edification or sermons. Actual moral inability or immorality are, as a rule, hidden in didactic moral edification. Teachers by their status (like parents toward children) often resort to the tool of moralizing, and they believe they can teach anything. But the possessors of evil think so as well. Moralizing is a peculiar professional disease of teachers. Moral terror underestimates personal good will. Its essence lies in making people happy coercively by imposing legitimized moral norms by stiff external regulation. Moral terror most often arises from paternalist relations and is typical of traditionalist structures. Even under the most democratic forms of education, teacher-student relations retain elements of authoritarianism. As such, these relations are favorable ground for moral terror.

Thus the concept of moral education, if literally interpreted as teaching morality, is inadequate. It is impossible to teach morality as though it were a classroom subject. This concept manifests the need of a society to influence the process of moral development, which ultimately is individual and, in general, spontaneous. Speaking about school practice, the process of moral education is likely very close, if not identical, to the educational process in general. It is realized through understandings about the substance and the method of education and through teachers' attitudes toward their business.

However, besides the above broad understanding of moral education there is a more specific understanding of it as training in the norms of public proprieties, as determined by culture and differing from society to society and within every nation. We see these as forms of individual behavior, including conduct at dinner and modes of worship. These forms of behavior are fixed in certain norms that set the criteria of right and wrong, of good manners in general. These are norms of decency, politeness, and etiquette. Confucius called them "ritual." They accustom a person to look at himself or herself reflectively, to have self-respect and respect for others. The right and proper behavior, good manners — capaciously called good breeding, individual culture — should not be confused with ethics (virtue), but actually are its necessary and reliable basis. The decent and polite person is opposed to the unsociable and rude one, the boor. There are cultures wherein "good breeding" is stressed more than in others. In traditional societies the norms of decent behavior were strictly codified; in modern society they tend to be washed away and individualized. Good breeding, like virtue, is not an innate feature of the individual. However, if virtue is formed non-didactically and latently, then good breeding mainly depends on overt as well as expedient educational efforts and can become a matter of training, of regulated pedagogical influence.

I have attempted to describe some salient changes in the Russian system of education — the expulsion of Marxist doctrinairism, the incorporation of new humanistic subjects, the development of academic liberties, the appearance of private educational institutions, and so on. These changes are matters of public concern today, because they signal major changes that mark the transformation of this region's system of education from an authoritarian regime to a democratic one. However, these changes will not solve another very important and difficult question regarding the new content of education, namely, maintaining a new and up-to-date paradigm that meets the needs of modern society as information-intensive, post-industrial, and post-traditional capitalist. But, perhaps needless to say, this is not exclusively a Russian problem.

# Education and the Quest for Democracy in South Africa

## BY HAROLD HERMAN

The demand for democracy has become strong and worldwide. So also did this demand pressure the undemocratic, apartheid state in South Africa over the past two decades. In 1990 a dramatic political shift started in the country, culminating in April 1994 with the first democratic, non-racial elections based on the principle of universal suffrage. An important question being asked is what kind of democratic order may develop in South Africa given its pluralistic nature, racial tensions, and political and economic divisions.

Samuel Huntington sees the world as experiencing its third wave of democratization. The first occurred from the late 18th century to 1926 when the United States and Western Europe become democratic; the second from 1943 to 1962 in West Germany, Italy, Japan, and India. The third wave began in 1974 in Portugal, Spain, Greece, and Latin America. These countries have become democracies after undergoing a transition process that was often painful, even traumatic, but that ultimately succeeded in bringing about a democratic system. South Africa is seen to be in a similar situation, in the throes of a process that displays remarkable similarities with those that Spain and Brazil experienced on the way to democracy. Hence the conclusion that South Africa also will become a democracy, in line with international trends. Key determinants for this change are whether suitable prerequisites or conditions exist and what the dynamics of the transition process will be (Giliomee 1992).

This essay explores the role that education has played in the drive for democracy in South Africa, the possibilities of a democratic state perhaps different from the liberal Western model, and the future role of education in shaping a democratic order.

## The Rise and Fall of the Undemocratic Apartheid State

The arrival of the Dutch settlers in 1652 started a process of white domination of the indigenous Khoisan and other African peoples, which continued with the advent of British colonial rule in 1806 and the establishment of the Union of South Africa in 1910. In the 20th century the oligarchic rule of the white minority population intensified dramatically despite black opposition and the reported acceptance of liberal-democratic values by a fair proportion of the ruling British and European settler elites. This type of rule was buttressed by good economic growth through exploitation of the country's vast mineral resources in an effective wealth-generating form of racial capitalism. The apartheid state created a perfect fit for the hierarchical labor relations on which capitalism thrives, with economic dependency characterized by center-periphery economic relations in favor of colonial exploitation by the United Kingdom and Western Europe. In these good economic times the continued expansion of apartheid policies to a crude form of institutionalized racism was thus possible in the period between 1948 and the 1970s, despite the intensified anti-apartheid struggles of the black majority and massive international opposition to these oppressive policies.

In the mid-1970s a social crisis was increasingly confronting the South African state. The salient features of the crisis were economic stagnation, the resurgence of black labor militancy, the Soweto students' uprising of 1976, intensified international pressure on the regime to abandon apartheid, and the shifts in the balance of power in the subcontinent following the collapse of the Portuguese empire (Davies 1986). The forces opposing apartheid and wishing to create a just, democratic, and non-racial society intensified significantly in the late 1970s and the 1980s. The South

African government and big business had to reassess their policies of racial segregation and economic exploitation.

On 2 February 1990 the State President, F.W. de Klerk, made a crucial policy speech at the annual opening of parliament in which he admitted the wrongs of the apartheid system, the need to move toward a non-racial democracy in South Africa, and the need of a universal franchise. But he also pointed out the need to protect individual and group rights. Bans on such political organizations as the African National Congress, the Pan Africanist Congress, and the South African Communist Party were lifted; and political prisoners, notably Nelson Mandela, were released. The government realized the need for a negotiated political settlement and a new constitution. Many of the legislative pillars of apartheid were scrapped. An era of social, political, economic, and educational reconstruction started. The long journey to a non-racial, non-discriminatory society, hopefully with justice and democratic values as its cornerstones, had begun.

## The Apartheid Legacy of Underdevelopment and Inequality

The massive social engineering of apartheid has tended to disguise the fact that South Africa is a Third World country with many of the manifestations of underdevelopment found in other countries in Africa and elsewhere.

In common with the rest of sub-Saharan Africa, South African education faces fiscal constraints and demographic pressures. The current total population is slightly above 36 million with 10.1 million pupils, of which 80% are African, in primary and secondary schools. Pressure on schools is rising because of the high African population growth of 2.8% each year (South African Institute of Race Relations 1989). This means that within five or six years there will be an estimated additional one million children reaching school age each year.

South Africa suffers from a low general level of education. Education is neither free nor compulsory for most children, and the adult functional literacy rate is only 50% (Hofmeyer and Moulder 1988). The education profile of the working population is typical of a developing country: 30% have no schooling, 36% have primary schooling only, and 31% have secondary schooling. Only 3% have degrees and diplomas. The stark inequalities in white, Indian, Coloured, and African education are clearly illustrated in Table 1 (Hofmeyer and Buckland 1992).

### Table 1

|  | White Education | Indian Education | Coloured Education | African Education |
|---|---|---|---|---|
| Pupil-teacher ratios | 17:1 | 20:1 | 23:1 | 38:1 |
| Underqualified teachers (less than std.10 plus a 3-year teacher's certificate | 0% | 2% | 45% | 52% |
| Per capita expenditure, including capital expenditure (in Rands) | 3,082.00 | 2,227.01 | 1,359.78 | 764.73 |
| Std. 10 pass rate | 96% | 93.6% | 72.7% | 40.7% |

NOTE: Std.10 - National school-leaving examination after twelve years of formal schooling

African children in the Bantu homelands and other rural areas are even more educationally disadvantaged than those in the common and urban areas. Some 24% of the Department of Education and Training's African pupils are in farm schools in rural areas (Gordon 1991). A mere 3% of the total of 5,782 rural schools offer education beyond standard five (grade seven), and 21% do not offer education higher than standard two (grade four).

The unequal distribution of natural resources in South Africa is a key factor in the debate on a future democratic society. Whites constitute only about 7.2% of the total population but at present own most of the mineral wealth and 87% of the land. In terms of distribution of resources, South Africa is one of the most unequal societies in the world. The Gini Coefficient, measuring the inequality between a country's rich and poor, is 0.66 for South Africa, the highest of the 57 countries in the world for which statistics existed in 1978 (Wilson 1990). Poverty and unemployment are widespread and rising to alarming proportions. The proportion of the total population living below subsistence (measured as the urban minimum living level) is estimated to be above 50% (Wilson 1990). Here lies one of the biggest challenges for a new democratically elected government: the redistribution of resources and wealth under the pressure of rising popular expectations. Thus South Africa faces the classic dilemma of many Third World societies in transition: how to foster social justice and equity without causing a drop in economic growth (Hawkins 1982).

For a democratic education structure and delivery system to evolve, for example, along the lines of the education policy of the largest liberation movement, the African National Congress, there are certain key prerequisites in the sociopolitical arena. A stable, lasting political settlement to solve the constitutional impasse is crucial. If it succeeds, then the potential is there for the South African economy once more to attract substantial foreign capital, to regain its former strength, and to reverse the current negative growth rate. The economy has been performing poorly for some time. The average growth rate has been less than 2% per annum since 1974, and the country's per capita income has declined by 0.5% annually and by more than 1% since 1981. The economy must grow by at least 5% annually in order to accommodate the 350,000 or more people who will enter the labor market each year during the rest of the 1990s (Hawkins 1982).

## Equality as Fundamental Goal of Democracy

C.B. MacPherson (1966) distinguishes between what he calls the old and new dimensions of democracy. Unlike the Western liberal democracies, the non-liberal democracies in newly independent underdeveloped countries traditionally tended to rate equality and community more highly than individual freedom. That factor makes the criterion of democracy the achievement of ends that the mass of the people share and that are put ahead of separate individual ends. This is the pre-liberal notion of democracy with strong

177

echoes of Rousseau, as found in many of the theoretical statements made by leaders of underdeveloped countries. Like Rousseau, they find the source of their social ills, moral depravity, dehumanization, and loss of freedom in inequality. Dignity, freedom, and humanity are to be achieved by re-establishing the equality that had been forcibly or fraudulently taken from them (MacPherson 1966).

The previous analysis showed just how underdeveloped and unequal South African society is. The popular demand for educational equality by the disadvantaged black majority will be relentless and vociferous because of the huge disparities between the deprived black educational model and the elite, continually visible white model. The South African government realized this and in 1983 committed itself to the notion of separate but equal quality education for all inhabitants.

A quarter of a million new pupils have entered the African education system each year, and more than 20,000 classrooms have been built during the past eight years. The pupil-teacher ratio in African schools has improved to 36:1 in both primary and secondary schools in 1989 from ratios of 55:1 in primary and 62:1 in secondary schools in 1981. Expenditure on education increased to 20% of the 1991-92 national budget. However, the white per capita expenditure is still some four times greater than that for Africans. In 1986 the government announced a Ten Year Plan with the aim of bringing about equal quality education for all by increasing the amount spent on education by 4.1% annually. However, in 1989 the Minister of National Education announced that the Ten Year Plan could no longer be met because of lack of economic growth. Given the economic realities in South Africa, the chances are remote that education expenditure in a future dispensation can exceed 20% of the budget.

Most political groups in the country realize that financial resources are finite and that there are distinct limits to the extent to which educational equality can be implemented. Recent policy changes by the government and its opposition show an acceptance that basic education, adult literacy and numeracy, and nine or 10 years of free, compulsory schooling for all children is probably the limit of free schooling that is possible, with more prudent state expenditure on senior secondary and postsecondary education.

## Education as an Instrument for Struggle and Transformation to a Democratic Society

The experience in many countries has shown that education has limited power to advance the cause for changing the status quo. In varying degrees, this also has been true of schooling in South Africa.

Up to the mid-1970s the policy of separate and unequal schooling for blacks was never seriously at risk, in spite of much opposition on the part of the black community. Apartheid in education persisted despite the opposition of liberation movements and progressive organizations to Bantu or "gutter" Education, Coloured Education, and the enforced Afrikaner Calvinist policies of Christian National Education. Some reasons for this persistence were the immense power of the regime, the strength of the economy, effective control by the education bureaucracy, the relative security and prosperity of civil servants and teachers, the effectiveness of divide-and-rule policies, and the repressive state security apparatus and the resulting limitations placed on mass mobilization and trade union power.

Until the mid-1980s most theories of Bantu Education — in other words, separate education for Africans — were seeking to explore the intersection of race, class, and education. They developed an approach based on a conception of the relation of education, capitalism, and apartheid. The articles in a 1984 collection edited by Peter Kallaway present this approach. The central argument is that South African education has to be understood chiefly in terms of the needs of the dominant capitalist class. The contention advanced is that in a capitalist society, education is not a means of social mobility, as argued by liberal critics of apartheid, but an important mechanism of the reproduction of capitalist relations of production and hence of the crystallization of class divisions.

Unterhalter and Wolpe (1991) contend that education is accorded immense and unwarranted weight as a mechanism either of social reproduction or social transformation, depending on the specific theoretical or political approach adopted. According to them, education is granted this privileged role in a variety of ways, for example, as the mechanism for the reproduction of the racial order and relations of production, or for the transformation of the system of social stratification and the redistribution of occupational opportunities. They advance the argument that education may be a necessary condition for certain social processes, but it is not a sufficient condition and hence cannot be analyzed as an autonomous social force. From the standpoint of the struggle for social transformation, the importance of this conclusion is that the structures and processes of educational change must be linked to changes in other social conditions and institutions.

Whatever one's theoretical position, it is a fact that since 1976 education has been a key site of the struggle for democracy in South Africa. Its limited effect on social change was reversed by the Soweto schools riots of that year, and democratic struggles became a powerful force of resistance and reform of Bantu Education. Between 1980 and 1986 there were widespread student protests and boycotts throughout the country. Despite harassment, pupils, university students, parents, and teachers organized and mobilized against Bantu Education. Student protests centered on such issues as control of schools and opposition to the Department of Education and Training controlling most African schools. Other key demands were the right to have democratically elected Student Representative Councils (SRCs) and Parent-Teacher-Student Associations (PTSAs), adequate physical facilities, and free textbooks. The authority of the state and its educational bureaucracy was severely challenged — and the crisis deepened.

## People's Education as a Force for Democratization

During the period from 1976 to 1980 the demands of black pupils shifted from an initial rejection of Afrikaans as the language of instruction to a demand for equal, free, and compulsory education. The continued intransigence of the government's discriminatory education policies and the refusal to meet black aspirations for democratic rule evoked extreme anger in young black people. Between 1980 and 1985 the cries of anger and protest of black pupils changed to the slogan, "liberation now, education later." Although understandable in its context, this view was impractical and ill-founded as a strategy and unhelpful to the struggles of the mass democratic movement. Revolutionary anger also was fueled by the declaration of a state of emergency in 1985 and the banning of the Congress of South African Students (COSAS). Student calls went out for a total boycott of classes and examinations in 1986. There was a widely held attitude, described by some as "immediatism," that the imminent collapse of apartheid was at hand; and there were calls for 1986 to become the "year of no schooling."

It was in this context that the Soweto Parents' Crisis Committee was formed in 1985 and a decision made to call a national consultative conference to devise a strategy to consolidate the gains made up to that point and to move the education struggle forward. The conference led to the formation of the National Education Crisis Committee (N.E.C.C.) in March 1986. The general feeling among teachers was that they recognized the importance of the school boycott but that students must prepare themselves for a useful role in society. It was felt that this could not be done by sacrificing education (Kruss 1988). The African National Congress in Lusaka was consulted, and they concurred that it was essential for young people to continue their education without giving up the struggle to end apartheid.

The call for "People's Education for People's Power" was made to use the schools as bases for People's Education. It would be a deliberate attempt to move away from reactive protests and to develop a counter-hegemonic strategy by laying a basis for a future, post-apartheid South Africa.

People's Education (P.E.) attempts to make explicit the links between education and political, economic, and cultural reproduction. It represents a shift from reactive responses to a more serious questioning of the nature of education itself. Kruss explains P.E.

in the following ways: Based on decades of education resistance, People's Education is a rejection of Apartheid Education, which is education for domination. It has an underlying assumption that education and politics are linked and, consequently, that the struggle for an alternative education system cannot be separated from the struggle for a non-racial, democratic South Africa. "People's Education for People's Power" is thus at the same time an educational and a political strategy. Through People's Education, people will be mobilized and organized toward the goal of a non-racial democratic South Africa; but at the same time, through People's Education people are beginning to develop a future education system (Kruss 1988).

People's Education as an education system, according to Kruss, must be controlled by and advance the interests of the mass of the people. Arising out of the education crisis, P.E. initially addressed itself to formal, school-based education. However, P.E. is intended to educate and empower all students, not only those in school. It must instill such democratic values as cooperative work and active participation, in opposition to current authoritarian and individualistic values dominant in schools. It must stimulate creativity and critical thinking to equip students for the future. Educational practices implementing the principles need to be developed by teachers (Kruss 1988).

The arenas in which P.E. hoped to be meaningful were diverse. One of its aims was to formulate an alternative, school-based education and to extend community control over education by establishing a people's authority alongside the existing state authority.

English, Mathematics and People's History commissions were set up to work on developing alternative curricular material and resources and to run alternative programs with parents and teachers outside of schools. However, they have thus far had a limited positive effect on schooling. The role of teachers is crucial for the implementation of P.E. This is a difficult task, however, because teachers often are criticized from all sides and treated by the education bureaucracy as instruments of policy. They often find that their own training in the apartheid system of education ill-equips them for progressive, critical thinking and learning. In many areas the morale, confidence, and self-image of teachers is at a low ebb.

There are serious doubts about the prospects of implementing P.E. And there are few indications that it will move beyond the level of political rhetoric. Soudien and colleagues (1989) raise serious questions as to how P.E. will be able to face problems relating to certification of pupils and to address the inevitable links between certification and employment.

Neville Alexander (1986) pointed out that it would be naive to think that an "alternative education system" could be set up as long as the apartheid state lasted and that, at most, it could only encroach on the control, content, and methodology of education within the schools. The Teachers League of South Africa, in its *Teachers Journal* of January-February 1988, expressed reservations about the concept of People's Education. It stated in an editorial that the ideas that "People's Education for People's Power" had produced to that point had proved almost wholly inadequate and off the mark.

Likewise, at the Research on Education in South Africa (RESA) conference held at Grantham, England, in March 1989, some reservations were expressed about P.E. on the grounds of:

- lack of clarity over precisely what it means and theoretical imprecision over the concepts "the people" and "the community";
- lack of consensus over the precise content of P.E.;
- the fact that not only state repression, but also headmasters, teachers, and school inspectors will block the move toward P.E.; and
- if P.E. is to contribute to a more just society, it will have to move beyond the common formula for mass education to an understanding of how reform in education is related to a fundamental redistribution of power, wealth, and privilege in society.

By the early 1990s the People's Education movement had lost some of its force and direction, not only for the reasons already mentioned but also because events around the political transition to democracy had diluted some of its ideological fervor. Jake Gerwel, a strong supporter of People's Education for People's Power in the 1980s, concurs that it did not progress as was hoped but that the concept remained politically and educationally to inform thinking and action (Gerwel 1990). One of the key contributions of the People's Education movement has been to place civil society structures, as opposed to state structures, high on the agenda regarding the centralization and decentralization of education in the post-apartheid era.

## Centralization and Decentralization of Schooling in the Quest for Democracy

Centralization of control has been a contentious issue in the history of South African education throughout this century. Considerable centralized control over all education enabled the state to keep a tight grip on education policy and practice. However, this has never been total because of structural, political, and resource constraints. Wirt and Harman (1986) point out that the reality of centralized control in developing countries is far from absolute; it breaks down in the provinces or regions because of value conflicts, poor infrastructure, and limited resources.

The racially exclusive departments, the provinces, and the Bantu homelands have resulted in an excessive fragmentation of South African education. There are 19 education departments in all, 11 in African education, which has produced administrative chaos and prevented the implementation of a single national policy on any matter (Selfe 1990). Because of the deliberate fragmentation of apartheid education to the advantage of the white community, the popular cry of the black majority has been for one ministry of education. The government finally accepted this in 1991, and since February 1993 there has been only one Minister of National Education, though the separate departments still exist.

Since the 1980s there has been substantial movement to privatize and decentralize control. Thus, for example, in order to counter the policy — politically unacceptable to the white electorate — of spending cuts for the four white provincial education departments (which would make the goal of racial equity more feasible), the government has increased local parental control of white primary and secondary schools. Four school models now exist for white parents among private schools and schools with varying degrees of state funding and parental control. Parents can have full control over admissions policies and the running of the schools, but with state funding limited to teachers' salaries. The ideological shift to increased community participation in schools clearly is intended to ensure that in a new, equitable system of resource allocation, white schools can retain control of their excellent facilities and experienced teaching corps.

According to Margaret Archer (1979) the degree and nature of centralization is the most crucial structural issue in education systems. The need to implement far-reaching education reforms that any new, democratically elected government will have to initiate in order to earn and retain legitimacy also will drive any new state toward centralization of control. Weiler (1990-91) argues that the large-scale decentralization of power is largely incompatible with the manifest interests of a modern state in maintaining effective control. He suggests that while decentralization can bring with it additional resources from communities, it also can produce inefficiencies that cancel out the benefits of additional resources. He also claims that the demand for uniformity and standardization implicit in modern technology and technological production tend to counteract centrifugal tendencies in curriculum policy. And he asserts that the main means of centralized control of the curriculum is through the examination and evaluation system.

The most significant motivation for decentralization, according to Weiler, is the use of decentralization to defuse and disperse conflict and reinforce the legitimacy of the state. According to Hofmeyer and Buckland (1992) all of these processes are evident in the South African situation. On the one side, there is the demand for centralization to enable policy changes for a democratic, equitable, unfragmented post-apartheid system of schooling. On the other side, there is a call for decentralized control from oppressed groups seeking greater democratic input into the policy process. A typical example of this is the call for Parent-Teacher-Student Associations by the representatives of the mass democratic movement and from privileged groups seeking to gain control over their privileged access to limited resources.

A new state probably would seek to centralize control to establish its power base and effectively implement policies of redress and equity in the current racially unequal system of schooling. This will have to be balanced against the need to earn greater legitimacy in terms of the rhetoric of democracy and the need to grant more power to communities and the private sector if they are to make greater contributions to the costs of education. This conflict, according to Hofmeyer and Buckland (1992), is likely to be articulated through the concepts of "civil society" and "community education," and there is already a powerful struggle over the meaning of these terms.

## Current Education Reform and Policies of Key Political Formations

After initial reluctance and incremental change, the South African government has accepted the inevitable, a unitary state, a nonracial, democratic system of government, and a universal franchise. One single Ministry of Education has been announced, as well as acceptance of the goal of equality of educational opportunity. In June 1991 a discussion document, *Educational Renewal Strategy*, was issued by the Department of National Education. It was revised after analysis and critique of the proposals, and in November 1992 a second document was released. The main goals of this wide-ranging plan to renew and restructure the education system are:

1. One democratic, non-racial education system, with both a central education authority and regional education authorities, that is to promote national unity while providing for particu-

lar religious, language, and cultural needs, in line with a new constitutional dispensation.

2. Equal educational opportunities and the elimination of backlogs in education facilities.
3. Relevant education at all levels and wide-ranging opportunities by means of extensive distance education delivery systems, better use of education technology, and liaison between the vocational training sector and formal education.
4. Basic adult education, especially for illiterate adults, and opportunities for lifelong education.
5. Greater management autonomy for education institutions and greater community involvement.
6. An extended role for technical colleges, the establishment of community colleges, and effective teacher education.
7. Greater mobility of learners between different education institutions or subsystems of the education system.
8. Adequate postsecondary education and financing for it.
9. Greater harmony between workforce needs of the country and educational opportunities.
10. An efficient, though adaptable, financing plan for education for the next 15 years.

This plan has been met with guarded optimism. The plan meets most of the fundamental needs articulated by the mass democratic movement over the years. However, education and politics are inseparable in South Africa, and the education strategy for change hinges on a political settlement and the implementation of a democratic constitution for the country.

At the same time as the *Educational Renewal Strategy* document was prepared, the National Education Coordinating Committee — established from the education sector of the broad, mass, democratic movement — commissioned an education policy analysis, the National Education Policy Investigation (NEPI). The NEPI report, dated 1992 but released in February 1993, sketches comprehensive policy options for a future educational dispensation.

Until the establishment of a new and more legitimate government after April 1994, education was in an uneasy transition period. This has been likened by Lee and Morphet (1989) to the Gramscian interregnum: "The crisis consists precisely from the fact that the old is dying and the new cannot be born; in this interregnum a great variety of morbid symptoms appear." Thus they believe that during the transition, opportunities will emerge to challenge, negotiate, and take risks, as the government's political will to maintain "the old" breaks down under pressure. Although a government of national unity took office after the first democratic elections in April 1994, educational changes cannot happen overnight; and many features of the "old" system will continue in the future.

## Constraints in the Transition to Democracy

At present the main factor bedeviling the transition to democracy is the high level of political intolerance and political violence currently prevailing in South Africa. The lifting of the ban on political organizations, the re-establishment of the right of free political organization and expression, and contests between the major political power groups in the country have unleashed politically inspired violence of unprecedented proportions, mostly black-on-black. The two major adversaries are the Zulu Natal-based Inkatha Freedom Party and the African National Congress, the largest liberation movement.

There has been a great deal of rhetoric about democracy in the transition stage to a post-apartheid dispensation. However, there is much yet to be learned about its practice. Hartshorne (1992) contends that it is not only the government that is finding it difficult to learn the lessons of democracy, but also the opposition groups are finding it difficult to develop a culture of democracy among their followers. Violence, intolerance, and intimidation are widespread in black communities; and, as black journalists are experiencing, freedom of speech can be a dangerous luxury. It is going to be a hard road to the achievement of a truly democratic state and society.

The structures of democracy are necessary but not sufficient in themselves. Beyond a democratic constitution, the rule of law, and the mechanisms of universal suffrage, there must be an acceptance by the people of South Africa of the values and culture of democracy. In the end, democracy is a way of thinking and behaving, a way of working and interacting with others in society. Critical to its survival is the exercise of tolerance, the right of independent judgment, the right of dissent, the capacity to discuss and negotiate, the use of rational argument rather than rhetoric, slogans, and intimidation.

Education has a key role to play in fostering these democratic values in a country where the vast majority of the population (50% adult functional illiteracy and 30% of children with no schooling) has historically been disadvantaged. Through the social engineering of apartheid, South Africa has a unique First World-Third World dichotomy with, at present, a highly educated sector of society with excellent teachers and education infrastructure (mostly white) and a large educationally disadvantaged sector (mostly black). Democracy and the democratic spirit can flourish only where there is an educated and informed citizenry and where education itself is democratic in spirit and practice. The challenge is to create this informed citizenry by using the substantial existing, albeit racially based, education infrastructure to the benefit and uplifting of all children and adults who have been denied educational opportunity in the past.

Hartshorne (1992) believes that it is vital that, in the next five to 10 years, energy should not be wasted in trying to "rescue" the present system of schooling or in trying to preserve the privileged position of some sectors within it. All the actors, including the educators who advise those who make the decisions, should direct their energy, intellect, imagination, and will to the practical planning of an education system consistent with a democratic, unitary, non-racial, and just South Africa. It will be comparatively easy to create the structures that will be necessary; but to create "new" teachers, "new" bureaucrats, "new" democratic citizens, and to transform their values, attitudes, and behavior, to step up quality and relevance in the classroom will be more difficult and demanding.

The second severe constraint to a smooth transition to democracy is the increasing militancy of black youth. Since the 1976 Soweto student protests, students continuously have launched campaigns of protest marches and class boycotts in the struggle against Bantu education. The number of educated unemployed has exacerbated the problem of youth lawlessness and intolerance. In 1981 the National Manpower Commission indicated that 59% of Africans and 66% of Coloureds under the age of 30 were unemployed. This position has worsened with the deepening economic recession. Bundy (1986) mentions four factors underlying the youth component of the massive confrontations of 1985:

- the glaring defects of black education;
- the substantial expansion of black schooling over the past few decades;
- unemployment among black school leavers; and
- the way in which organizational capacity and experience have transformed consciousness.

The militancy of black youth has caused great concern over the past decade. Brian O'Connell (1989) discusses various aspects of youth power in schools and colleges. Calls are continually going out to school children in Soweto and other black urban areas from the mass democratic movement — and from teachers, parents, and political parties — to return to school. Many schools are not functioning at all. P. Molefe (1993) contends that black education is sitting on a time bomb as pupil power gets out of hand. He says that the aphorism that "power tends to corrupt and absolute power corrupts absolutely" most certainly applies to the students of today, bold as they are in their ability to impose terms on education authorities, teachers, and the community at large. This is a very disturbing aspect of the struggle for democracy in the schools, and one can only hope that a negotiated political settlement will lead to the rehabilitation of what is now commonly referred to as an angry, lost generation of young people.

## The Future Democratic State and the Role of Education

There is little doubt that the move toward democracy and education change in South Africa will be in the direction of being more just, equitable, non-racial, and democratic. This is confirmed by analysis of the education policies outlined by liberation movements, such as the African National Congress. John Samuel (1992) outlines the latter's educational aims in a policy paper in which clear goals are set for democratic education, the development of human potential, the role the state should play in achieving those goals, and the equitable distribution of resources.

The key question is what kind of democracy South Africa will opt for in the next decade. South Africa has been an enigma to political analysts, and many past predictions on the transformation of the society have been palpably wrong. Current predictions about the nature of the future democratic state also may be wrong, if it is democratic at all.

According to C.B. MacPherson's (1966) categories, the underdevelopment variant of non-liberal democracy has emerged strongly in post-colonial Africa. One is inclined to place South Africa in this category, as well.

This kind of democracy, according to MacPherson, though adopted more recently, seems to go directly back to the old notion of democracy that predates Marx and predates the liberal state — the notion of democracy as rule by and for the *oppressed* people. Liberal democracies have a direct link with capitalist, industrial economic systems. Since the underdeveloped nations had, on the whole, simpler cultures than those who dominated them, it is not surprising that they resorted to a concept of democracy that goes back to a simpler pre-industrial society.

Democracies in underdeveloped states have tended to reject the competitive market society as something imposed on them from outside or from above. Also, in Africa they have tended to opt for single-party systems of government, which are foreign to the liberal notion of democracy. South Africa differs from democracies in the underdeveloped variant in that capitalist economic relations

191

are firmly entrenched and the free market operates, albeit predominantly in favor of a privileged white minority. The capitalist consciousness is firmly entrenched, even among the black working class, who aspire to the goods that racial capitalism has denied them. Peter Berger (1992) also sees a clear link between liberal democracy and capitalism, and he has drawn heavy criticism from the Marxist left for his views on liberal democracy and its links with capitalism, as well as for his skepticism about democratic socialism.

South Africa has every chance of establishing a multi-party democracy different from the communist or underdeveloped variant. The main reason for the difference is the strong capitalist base of the economy and the world tide against communism and socialism. The failure of socialist policies in Tanzania, Zambia, and Zimbabwe and the failure of Mozambique and Angola to develop a stable society mitigate against a socialist future with, at most, a social market economy in South Africa. Even committed Marxist-Leninists of the South African Communist Party now have accepted the idea of the market, a mixed economy, minimum nationalization, and multi-party elections. The pervasiveness of world capitalism and the strong resurgence of the World Bank and International Monetary Fund with economic structural-adjustment policies obviously have strongly affected the debate about a future economy and a democratic state.

The tough, extremist political rhetoric of some political groups a few years ago has been toned down substantially; and there has been increased dialogue and even consensus between the South African government, the liberation movements, and other political parties in the run-up to the first democratic election. An agreement on an interim government of national unity/power sharing (the parties differ on terminology) was struck between the Nationalist Party government and the African National Congress during February 1993. This agreement was followed by consultations with other political groups for a multi-party forum for negotiations on a new constitutional dispensation. Multi-party elections are to be held in April 1994 to constitute an interim government of national unity based on proportional representation. It will negotiate changes to the interim constitution achieved by consensus between parties. The next election has to be held within five years under the final constitution agreed to during this period.

These are dynamic times for education in South Africa, and it faces huge challenges as it contributes meaningfully to a democratic future.

## References

Alexander, N. "Ten Years of Educational Crisis: The Resonance of 1976." Paper presented at the conference on "Education for Affirmation," Broederstroom, 1986.

Archer, M.S. *Social Origins of Educational Systems*. London: Sage, 1979.

Berger, P. *Democracy and Capitalism in Development and Democracy*. Johannesburg: Urban Foundation, August 1992.

Bundy, C. "Schools and Revolution." *New Society* (January 1986).

Davies, J. "Crisis Education and Restructuring in South Africa." In *Capitalist Crisis in Schooling*, edited by R. Sharp. Sydney: MacMillan, 1986.

Department of National Education. *Education Renewal Strategy*. Pretoria, November 1992.

Gerwel, G.J. "The Road to Transformation of a University like MEDUNSA." Keynote address at the Students' Conference, Medical University of South Africa, July 1990.

Giliomee, H. "Towards Democracy." *Journal of the Institute for Multi-Party Democracy* 1, no. 3 (1992): 20.

Gordon, A. "South African Farm Schools: The Neglected Sector." Paper presented at the Farm Schools Networking Conference, Broederstroom, 1991.

Hartshorne, K. "Foreword." In *Education Alternatives*, edited by R. McGregor and A. McGregor. Cape Town: Juta, 1992.

Hawkins, J.N. "Educational Reform and Development in the People's Republic of China." In *Comparative Education*, edited by P.G. Altbacht et al. New York: Macmillan, 1982.

Hofmeyer, J.M., and Buckland, P. "Education System Change in South Africa." In *Education Alternatives*, edited by R. McGregor and A. McGregor. Cape Town: Juta, 1992.

Hofmeyer, J.M., and Moulder, J. "Towards Scenarios for South African Education: Trying to Find the Rules of the Game." *South African Journal of Higher Education* 2, no. 1 (1988): 9-13.

Kallaway, P., ed. *Apartheid and Education*. Johannesburg: Ravan Press, 1984.

Kruss, G. *People's Education in South Africa: An Examination of the Concept*. Bellville: Centre for Adult and Continuing Education, University of the Western Cape, 1988.

Lee, R.H., and Morphet, A.R. "Programmatic Evaluation of the Education Support and Training Project." Unpublished report. U.S.A.I.D. South Africa Mission, 1989.

MacPherson, C.B. *The Real World of Democracy*. Oxford: Oxford University Press, 1966.

Molefe, P. "Crisis in Education." *The Cape Town Argus*, 25 February 1993.

National Education Policy Investigation. *Report*. Cape Town: Oxford University Press, 1992.

O'Connell, B. "Education and Transformation: A View from the Ground." Paper presented at the Research on Education in South Africa conference, Grantham, U.K., 1989.

Samuel, J. "The A.N.C. View." In *Education Alternatives*, edited by R. McGregor and A. McGregor. Cape Town: Juta, 1992.

Selfe, J. "The Present Systems and the Dynamics Arising and Constraining Change: Current Flashpoints." Johannesburg: Urban Foundation, Feb. 1990.

Soudien, C., et al. "The Problems of Certification and People's Education." Paper presented at the conference of the Association of Sociologists of Southern Africa, 1989.

South African Institute of Race Relations. *Race Relations Survey 1988/89*. Johannesburg, 1989.

Unterhalter, E., and Wolpe, H. *Apartheid Education and Popular Struggles*. Johannesburg: Ravan Press, 1991.

Weiler, H. "An Exercise in Contradiction? Comparative Perspectives on Educational Decentralisation." *Educational Evaluation and Policy Analysis* (Winter 1990/91).

Wilson, F. "Poverty, the State and Redistribution: Some Reflections." In *The Political Economy of South Africa*, edited by N. Nattrass et al. Cape Town: Oxford University Press, 1990.

Wirt, F.M., and Harman, G. *Education Recession and the World Village: A Comparative Political Economy of Education*. London: Falmer Press, 1986.

# Education for Democracy in Japan and Asia

## BY WILLIAM K. CUMMINGS

In the contemporary world economy, Japan is no trivial player. Japan provides one-quarter of the world's productivity and one-third of its annual volume of investment. Moreover, the Japanese share of global economic activity is expanding steadily. Japan's economic prominence is thought to be a recent phenomenon; but, as Paul Kennedy reminds us, Japan already was a force by the turn of the 20th century. In 1905 it defeated Russia, and its economy was moving forward at an impressive rate. Japan was given a major place in the crippled League of Nations and was destined to broaden its global role. In that early period, many Asian leaders were looking to Japan for political and cultural leaders. Many of those who later led the revolutions in China and several Southeast Asian nations received part of their education in Japan.

Unfortunately, Japan chose to rely on the sword for the expansion of its global position and ultimately suffered an ignominious defeat. Japan was precipitously dropped from the world club formed by the victors. Perhaps equally unfortunate, the Japanese military forces damaged much of the goodwill that had been built up in previous decades. Korea was — and is — the exception, as Japan has never enjoyed much good will there. Japan's brutal colonization of Korea from the early years of the 20th century through 1945 left deep scars. Nevertheless, it also left a deep imprint on Korean institutions. Thus some of the structural and ideological generalizations I will make in my discussion of the Asian model also apply to Korea.

But over the more than four decades since the conclusion of World War II, Japan has re-emerged as a major global economic and cultural-ideological force and now is searching for a political role. Most Asian nations, while feeling considerable antipathy to Japan, nevertheless look with interest on the Japanese search. Many find that they share similar traditions and patterns of development with Japan. Hence they tend to be sympathetic to the positions taken by Japanese leaders.

A particular example is the nature of democracy and the importance of human rights. Most Asian nations, with Japan a notable exception (Burks 1985), have a somewhat despotic form of government that provides a limited, albeit expanding, role for the political opposition. The political leaders of these nations thus take exception to the recent shrill call from the West, through such Western-controlled institutions as the United Nations and Amnesty International, for universal conformity to Western notions of political, civil, and social rights. At a minimum, the Asian leaders resent the imposition of Western models by international organizations from which Asians are excluded. Also, the Asian leaders question the merits of these Western models: If they are so good, why is the West in so much trouble?

This restrained voice of protest has been expressed in such forums as the recent meeting of nonaligned nations in Bandung. But more concretely, it is expressed through Japan's persistent push for a new political role in the current international order. Asian leaders look to Japan to articulate the "Asian model" of democracy. Thus in writing about Japan today and its experience with education and democracy, I also want to explore this notion of an Asian model. To do so requires a brief journey into Japanese and Asian thinking about core concepts and a review of the evolution of Japanese political institutions, which only recently have become firmly committed to democracy.

## Conceptual and Historical Background

*Defining Terms.* Democracy takes many forms and can occur at many different levels in the social system. In the Western tradition, I sense that the prime focus of most discussions about democracy is the national polity. Does the polity guarantee political, civil, and social rights? Is it attracting high quality leadership? Should it rely on direct voting for high offices or selection through representation? Perhaps of most fundamental concern is the quality of the relation of individuals to the state.

Democracy in the West also is manifest in other institutions. There is an extensive literature that suggests that more democratically managed firms are more effective. The recent increase in women's involvement in the labor force has heightened interest in the democratic family. And commentators periodically take a careful look at labor institutions, nongovernmental organizations, local governments, and other institutions, wondering how democratic they are. But these are all side issues in Western, and especially American, discourse. Few thinkers or leaders seem to believe that democracy in one institutional setting — for example, the family — is requisite for democracy in another, that is, in the national polity. These linkages are not viewed as critical.

Particularly when we turn to education, the focus is on the democratic national polity. The curriculum and textbooks focus almost exclusively on the national polity. The textbooks and the teachers provide American youth with a cognitively based introduction to the birth of democracy in America and the West. For example, both of the papers in this volume focusing on civics in the American curriculum have a cognitive approach, differing only in whether the focus should be exclusively on the American experience or might better adopt a comparative approach. Meanwhile, the students are allowed no role in the governance of their schools or communities. For that matter, the teachers themselves are allowed only a modest role in the governance of their schools. Democracy is taught in a comparatively authoritarian setting.

The segmented Western approach of focusing on national institutions and narrowly featuring (cognitively based) civic education is greeted with incredulity by Japanese educators.* As we will see when we review the Japanese educational tradition, education

---

*A useful review of Japanese reactions to American education is found in George Bereday and Shigeo Matsui, *American Education Through Japanese Eyes* (Honolulu: University Press of Hawaii, 1973).

there is viewed as an integral part of the broader social and cultural order. Linkages between institutions are assumed. And how an individual thinks is considered to be closely related to what they feel and believe and to the support they receive from others. Thus, concerning many of the implicit but deep-seated assumptions of Western thinking and practice related to education for democracy, Japan provides a contrast.

The more holistic Japanese approach means not only that the non-cognitive dimensions of school education need to be in focus but also that educational experiences outside the school need to be considered. Thus Japanese discourse on democratic education also looks at family education, community and youth education, workplace education, and, perhaps most significantly, at the lessons conveyed by the news, media, and popular culture.

We also should note one other interesting theme that emerges in Western democratic discourse. Many of the great Western "democratic" reform efforts have focused on access to established education institutions, seeking to open the doors to minorities and the lower socioeconomic classes, first to primary school and later to secondary and higher education. The assumption is that a democratic society is one wherein the individual enjoys unobstructed opportunity to reap the full benefits of education and that education, in turn, enables access to full economic, social, and political participation. This line of thinking enables Western reformers to gain comfort merely from focusing on the doors. We suspect that the Japanese reformer (and more generally the Asian reformer) is inclined to direct more attention to what is inside those doors. The individual cannot achieve equal opportunity if the institutions are grossly unequal. Thus Japanese reform has focused more acute attention on the structure of relations within such institutions as the school, the family, and the workplace than has Western reform.

*Education in Pre-Democratic Japan.* Following the Meiji restoration (1868) Japanese education took a sharply Western shift. However, in time, negative reactions resulted in the resurrection of many earlier traditions. These traditions go back for centuries and can loosely be thought of as Shinto, Buddhist, and Confucian in origin. During the Tokugawa period they gained the form of consolidation that has the most direct bearing on the Meiji reforms. The Tokugawa regime has been characterized as centralized feudalism. A single warrior domain (*han*) was able to achieve dominance over some 250 others and establish a pattern of checks and balances that could be sustained for more than two centuries. Each of the 250 varied domains followed somewhat similar patterns of organization, by virtue of Tokugawa law and taxation; but they also enjoyed considerable autonomy. Following are some of the special characteristics of this period:

1. Heredity. The rulers of each domain were decided by a hereditary principle, father to son. Supreme councils existed in the domains to supervise the succession; and in cases where the eldest son was not fit, these councils identified worthy replacements. Consensus was the principle in these and other high-level decisions, with the *shogun* (for the Tokugawa domain) and the *daimyo* (for the other domains) having the first vote.

2. Stratification. The local societies were divided into an explicit caste system of samurai and commoners. The respective castes had different rights and received a different education. Within both strata, but especially the samurai class, women were accorded a limited role of being "good mothers and wise wives."

3. Moral Code. Confucian ethics prevailed as the standard of conduct for both strata. Thus virtue was the highest human quality and was viewed as the key to social stability and prosperity. Samurai were instilled with the ideal of virtue in domain schools (along with education in more practical skills, including military strategy and martial arts). Commoners were taught the importance of virtue by parents and often in local schools run by priests (*terakoya*).

4. Extensive Education. The best estimates are that the great majority of samurai, who constituted upwards of 5% of the

population, and easily one-third of the commoners achieved literacy. In total, some 40% of the male population and 20% of the female population were literate by the mid-19th century, prior to the modernizing Meiji restoration (Dore 1965).

5. The Imperial Institution. The great irony of the Tokugawa period was that the emperor, though the symbolic originator of the Japanese people, had no place either in the political institutions or in the education tradition. Yet the emperor was not forgotten, especially by certain critical intellectuals who searched for the sources of Japan's weakness.

*Education in Early Modern Japan.* Mounting economic troubles combined with the imminent threat of Western imperialism, as expressed by the "black ships" of Commodore Perry, led to extensive social turmoil and, finally in 1868, to what is now called the Meiji Restoration. A clever and energetic cadre of young (and mostly lower-ranking) samurai engineered a coup with such slogans as "Restore the Emperor" and "Expel the Barbarians." These revolutionaries decided to locate the new government in Tokyo (formerly Edo). Over the next several years they introduced an extraordinary array of reforms.

The greatest concern of the new leaders, who because of their teamwork style of rule came to be know as the Meiji oligarchs, was to rapidly develop in Japan the capacity to resist being colonized by the imperialistic West. They decided to invoke the symbol of the emperor as a basis for consolidating all power under a single central government. Thus, virtually overnight, they banished the numerous independent domains and set about developing a new centralized regime under their leadership, with the emperor as symbolic head.

Recognizing the strong and potentially violent opposition of the privileged samurai class, the reformers abolished this class, requiring all members to turn in their weapons. Meanwhile, the new government took rapid steps to strengthen its own military forces, modernize their weaponry, and expand their recruitment base so as to include commoners along with former samurai. This new army, whose leaders were given central places in the new government, provided an important threat against potential opposition during the period of state formation.

An important corollary of the abolition of feudal classes was the exhortation, as early as 1872, that every family was responsible for sending all of its children to school. Rapid steps were taken to develop a "modern" compulsory school system where children of all backgrounds were expected to sit side by side and experience a common curriculum,

These leaders had tremendous respect for the power of Western technology and sought through various means to gain mastery of this lore as rapidly as possible. They also believed that Western imperialists would seek to intervene if they did not, at least, make a pretense of adopting Western practice in areas such as governance, law, and finance. And so they took appropriate measures. Yet the majority view among the leaders was to preserve Eastern morality. Gradually this view prevailed. The Imperial Rescript on Education, promulgated in 1891, made clear the commitment to a familistic code of conduct reminiscent of the past. This code became the foundation spirit for the curriculum. Along with standard academic subjects, a special course on moral education was added to the primary and secondary levels (often taught by individuals who had completed military service). This course did not stress "education for democracy"; its primary emphasis was on social duty, with a significant dose of emperor worship. School leaders were encouraged to develop an overall educational experience supportive of Japanese values. Pictures of the emperor were placed in every classroom. Codes of behavior were established. Principals led daily school assemblies where moral lessons were imparted. Local school management practices were initiated where principals and teachers met daily for routine matters and weekly for deeper discussions of curricular and extracurricular issues, searching for ways to achieve full integration of the various elements of the educational experience in school and out.

At this period, most Western nations were ruled by representative bodies, and so the Japanese leaders felt some pressure to imitate that pattern. This can be seen in various early official statements, as well as in exhortations by key intellectuals. But gradually the leadership backed away. They placed considerable emphasis on the development of strong local governments, led by individuals (whom they appointed) who were both respected in the local areas because of large land holdings or other achievement and evidenced central loyalties. In the Meiji constitution, promulgated in 1889, the leaders outlined a form of government with a strong central leadership that would receive limited advice from a *diet* composed of members elected from an extremely narrow electoral base. Thus the constitution ushered in the form of democracy while preserving the reality of oligarchic control.

Over the next few years certain political groups formed into parties, based primarily on the strength of rival business combines. But at least through the first 20 years or so these parties exercised extreme caution in challenging the center. The national political groups were held together by the ability of key factional leaders to obtain funds from particular corporations. These leaders then would share the funds with the members of their faction in exchange for cooperation. The factional members would use these funds to reward their supporters at the local level. Thus from an early stage the pattern of boss-controlled and highly personalized politics was set. Politics was not about issues, but about candidates and money (Curtis 1988).

The growing influence of business in politics had its consequences for education policy. Increasingly, new education initiatives came to reflect the interests of this group. Thus higher professional schools were launched in the 1890s to supply business leaders with technical, commercial, and linguistic skills. And from the second decade of this century, a new group of single-faculty universities were established to increase the supply of engineers.

A final important feature of this period was Japan's drift toward imperialism, first taking on China in 1895 and then Russia in 1905. The latter victory was widely heralded in Asia as the first time an Asian nation had defeated a Western nation. But the downside was its encouragement to those in the Japanese oli-

garchy who were convinced that Japan's national strength de-
pended on the development of an empire. Over time, the views of
this latter group gained ascendancy, particularly as the Japanese
economy experienced the effect of the worldwide depression.

*Education in Wartime Japan.* The period from 1912 to 1926,
known as Taisho democracy, marked a fatal turning point for
Japan's political evolution. On one hand, some independent tendencies were emerging in the labor movement and among students, who, particularly following the Bolshevik revolutions, were
impressed by communism. On the other hand, the oligarchs and
business leaders were developing a concern about social anarchy
in the increasingly unstable international environment. Overall,
this was a period of prosperity stimulated by rapid advances in
industrialization and accompanied by an expansion of the middle
class. Also, there were some steps toward social liberalization.
The right of franchise was significantly expanded, and the private
sector was allowed new freedoms in various activities, including
education.

But at a certain point the bubble popped. The symbolic event
was the Showa restoration, the attempt by a young group of military officers to carry out a coup against the liberal party politicians
who had gained considerable influence in the national government. Gradually a pattern of suppression set in, and the aforementioned imperialistic policies gained ascendancy. Japan was
marching toward war, first against small countries in Asia, which
were to be included in the Greater East Asian Prosperity Sphere,
and later against the entire Allied Powers.

The militaristic shift was not unopposed. Established politicians with liberal views voiced their opposition, often at their
peril. A number of intellectuals bravely spoke or wrote against the
emerging policies, at the risk of being jailed. An underground
movement formed among intellectuals, often communist, who
abhorred the conservative shift. But none of these efforts to thwart
Japanese fascism was sufficient. The nascent democracy was
crushed by the determined military. Yet throughout this period the

shell of democracy was maintained; and if one can believe the autobiographies written later, many of those civilians who occupied high offices during this period retained their hope that somehow the military leaders would come to their senses and reverse the path toward world war and disaster.

In education the effect was certainly anti-democratic in tone. Yet it also was egalitarian. The military leaders, often recruited from rural areas, recognized that farm-born children were more likely to serve them well. Thus impressive steps were taken to strengthen rural education. Access at all levels of education was significantly improved, and rural youth often were the beneficiaries of new scholarship or tuition-free schemes. By the end of World War II, Japan had an extensive education system, equaling in scale those of Western Europe.

## Postwar Polity

The war left Japan devastated. More than 2 million soldiers and a half-million civilians had died as a direct consequence of the war effort. The economy was devastated. And whatever good will Japan once had enjoyed in Asia was expended.

But there also were some positive legacies. With the emperor's agreement to unconditional surrender, the people were relieved. It now became possible to admit that the militaristic effort was wrong and never should have been undertaken. A determination emerged to never repeat that adventure. Out of the embers of war was born a hunger for peace that was embodied in a new constitution formally prohibiting Japan from ever taking up arms for offensive purposes.

Those who had pushed the war were totally discredited, and those who had resisted were heroes. Thus the few liberals and leftists who had tried to stand in the way of the military machine gained new legitimacy, and this considerably increased their opportunity to advance their positions in the new postwar era.

Also, while much of Japan's infrastructure in various sectors was destroyed, the nation's human capacity had improved steadily. Education expanded rapidly throughout the postwar period. At least in terms of scale, education now was prepared to play a major role in the reconstruction of the new society.

Following Japan's formal surrender, the Allied powers formed an occupation government to oversee the transformation of Japanese society. The U.S. armed forces, which had been the major opponent of Japan in the Pacific theater, became the major actor in the Occupation; and General Douglas MacArthur was appointed as head of the effort. The reforms introduced were strongly influenced by American practice.

The Occupation's two initial goals were to demilitarize and democratize Japan. Economic reconstruction came later, when the Allied powers, following the loss of China, recognized that they would need a powerful Japan as an ally. Demilitarization proceeded rapidly, with the armies disbanded and weapons turned over within weeks. Key military institutions were stripped and closed down, and major figures in the war effort were identified for later prosecution by a controversial war tribunal.

Democratization was a more complicated process. The Occupation, relying on key Western advisors and consultation with selected Japanese leaders, entered into extended deliberations. As these were going on, steps were taken to open the political arena to all potential participants. Labor unions were recognized. The long-banned Communist Party was allowed to come out in public. Public employees, including teachers and professors, were allowed to organize. As the deliberations proceeded, the politicking of these various liberated groups was intense and colorful.

The new constitution, formally promulgated in 1946, was a major departure from its predecessor. The state was formed by citizens, rather than the emperor; and these citizens had rights, rather than duties. The rights were numerous and progressive. Women, for example, enjoyed equal rights to work; professors enjoyed the right of academic freedom; all adult citizens, regardless of gender or wealth, enjoyed the right to vote.

Possibly the most notable feature of the constitution was its prohibition of state use of military force for offensive purposes in the international arena. This feature led to the appellation, "Peace Constitution"; and Japan has adhered steadfastly to this stance from the Cold War period to the present. But Japan's peace policy has met objections from lingering conservatives in Japan and, ironically, from certain U.S. politicians who wanted Japan to rearm so that the U.S. could reduce its share of the Cold War defense burden.

The first elections, held soon after the constitution's announcement, drew an impressive voter turnout; but the result was a restoration of many old-system politicians to their seats in the Diet. However, a subsequent election in 1948 resulted in a victory by a coalition of leftist parties. It briefly appeared that Japan was headed into a new democratic era of competitive politics. But the leftist government proved inept and was promptly replaced by a conservative coalition. The conservatives have dominated every national election since.

The new constitution established an independent judiciary for the execution of criminal and civil justice. The subsequent record in these areas is impressive. Few people in the world feel as comfortable with the procedures in these areas as do the Japanese. Most court cases, at least at the lower levels, seem to be conducted impartially. The police system has a well-deserved reputation for honesty and competence.

In the social area, the constitution outlined bold promises in such areas as the right to work, welfare, health, education, and housing. The actual elaboration of the detailed programs has been largely the task of the political process, relying on the thoughtful advice of central bureaucrats. Of those several social areas, it might be said that Japan's record in work, health, and education is outstanding; however, its record in welfare and housing leaves much to be desired, at least by Western standards.

Japan's differential performance in social policy reflects a deep-seated belief, presumably of Confucian origin, that the state should wisely intervene in some areas — such as the provision of education and the promotion of economic growth — while avoiding excessive involvement in other areas — such as welfare and housing — where the private sector, and more specifically the family, has responsibility (Cummings 1989). Many leaders in Japan reason that developing strong social welfare and public housing programs encourages weak families. For example, when public housing becomes available, young people and young married couples may choose to live away from their parents, thus limiting their obligation to their parents as well as their responsibility to look after the parents when they are old and infirm.

Similarly, placing the burden for supporting health on families encourages the family members to be more health conscious. Of course, none of this is black and white. Especially concerning health policy, Japan has developed a very effective national health insurance system that, at relatively low cost, provides an effective backstop for those citizens who do not participate in corporate-sponsored programs. The important point is that, despite the constitutional guarantee of social rights, traditional values militate in certain areas against the development of programs that will secure these rights.

Distinct from promoting the concept of citizenship and of strengthening popular participation, the Occupation initially sought to decentralize the administration of public services. The assumption was that a shift of the locus of power and administration closer to the people would encourage more meaningful citizen involvement. Many of the powers of key central ministries were to be stripped. For example, what today is known as MITI (Ministry of International Trade and Industry) was to be essentially disbanded. And much of the decision-making of the Ministry of Education in such areas as curriculum, textbooks, appointments, salaries, and school construction was to be shifted to local governments run by locally elected politicians. Local governments also were to assume responsibility for the former national universities, thereby making them into analogs of the U.S. land-grant institutions.

But very soon into its tenure the Occupation abandoned most of these decentralizing reforms. Officials concluded that the reforms would be impossible to accomplish without relying on the estab-

207

lished centralized bureaucratic structures. However, outside of the public sector the Occupation was able to dismantle some of the old structures. For example, it forced a breakup of the old multisector cartels (*zaibatsu*), and it carried out an extensive purge of "war criminals." The Occupation also launched a massive land reform and introduced new labor regulations that significantly improved the position of organized labor and women workers.

*Postwar Democracy.* The structure of postwar national politics can be said to resemble the prewar pattern with the conservatives, closely aligned to big business, experiencing limited though occasionally vociferous resistance from a coalition of opposition parties. In effect, Japan has a one-and-a-half party system.

Within the conservative party, the organization is highly personalistic and factionalized: Politicians seem committed to alliances, not to ideas. Fueling the alliances is the money that the central politicians can collect from outside sources. The central politicians turn this over to the members of their factions, who, in turn, use the money to hold frequent parties and provide other benefits in their local areas. Politicians succeed to the extent that they can become popular with their constituency. Attributes of character, congeniality, and favor-giving stand a politician in good stead, rather than what he or she stands for.

This structure has interesting consequences for voter loyalty and behavior. Most voters seem to have, at best, lukewarm attachments to politics and politicians. The big challenge for politicians, especially in the case of national elections, is to get voters to turn out. It seems as though the level of voter apathy has increased over time. Particularly in recent years, that apathy has been replaced by disgust. Seemingly each week a new political scandal is uncovered. The Recruit insider stock-trading scandal was followed by the Kyubei Shipping Company pay-out. Major politicians from both parties have been implicated, leading to a new cry for reform of political funding and of elections. It is too early to suggest what may be the consequence of these developments. With the bad image they are giving the political establishment, it naturally can be asked, What is the appropriate reaction for an educator?

*"Miracle" Japan and the Postwar International Order.* It can be argued that the Occupation's failure to carry out major administrative reform was a blessing for Japan. In the absence of a highly effective or visionary political system, Japan's administrative elites often are credited with devising the policies that have encouraged vigorous and effective economic recovery. Through virtually every year of the postwar period, Japan's economic growth has significantly exceeded that of other industrial nations. Particularly during the 1960s, when the Japanese economy acquired the "miracle" label, average annual growth exceeded 10%.

During this miracle growth period, the economic leaders focused on the production of key goods primarily for the export market. Raw materials were sought from nearby Asian neighbors, converted into attractive export products, and exported to the West (primarily to the United States). This strategy enabled Japanese corporations to command handsome profits and rapidly build their capital, while at the same time expanding trade relations in a new Asian market. Gradually, Japan came to expand its involvement in Asia, increasing both trade and investments, thus giving birth to the Pacific Rim Economic Zone.

By the mid-1980s, Japan had become a major economic power with an economy second in scale only to the United States and with an unrivaled capacity for new capital investment. Whereas Japan had once been dependent on other parts of the world for capital and technology, now the tables were reversed. Leading industrial nations, including the United States, were heavily dependent on Japanese investments. The rising financial influence of Japan has led to several major policy questions that are noted here as a backdrop for our discussion of the possibility of an Asian model of education for democracy. Four questions are important:

1. As Japan's mercantilist policies pile up successes year after year by following the standard principles of free trade, other nations cry foul and ask Japan to voluntarily restrain exports. Should Japan do this? After all, Japan is following the rules of the game set by others.

2. Japan especially wonders why it should cooperate with these requests when it is not accorded full membership in the key international organizations of the postwar order. Why cooperate absent international respect?

3. To date, Japan's primary involvement in the postwar world is through its economic productivity. But economics alone may not be enough to gain respect. Does Japan need to develop a military capability before other nations will pay attention?

4. It may be that Japan has yet another message to convey, how to run a "good" society. The West's recent shrill advice on such matters as human rights is provocative, but how impressive really are human rights in the West? Might not the rights be excessive while the corresponding sense of responsibility is weak? Thus, overall, is not the quality of life in the West deficient? Many Japanese leaders believe that their nation has struck a better balance between rights and responsibilities than the leading Western societies.

## Democratic Education

Education reform was central to the Occupation's reforms.* Following the release of a report by a distinguished group of U.S. educators, the Occupation proceeded to introduce a series of changes that today are regarded by most historians as Japan's Second Educational Revolution. The cornerstone of these reforms is the *Fundamental Law of Education* of 1947, which spells out a new philosophy of education centered on the interests of the child, rather than the state:

> Education shall aim at the full development of personality, striving for the rearing of the people, sound in mind and body, who shall love truth and justice, esteem individual

---

*On K-12 school reforms, see William K. Cummings, *Education and Equality in Japan* (Princeton, N.J.: Princeton University Press, 1980); for reforms at the university level, see Cummings, *The Academic Marketplace and University Reform* (New York: Gardner, 1991).

value, respect labor, have a deep sense of responsibility, and be imbued with an independent spirit, as builders of a peaceful state and society.

The new education philosophy required a wholesale abandonment of the old curriculum and the wartime texts. Initially, private publishers were allowed to develop and promote whatever texts they wished, and local school districts enjoyed unrestricted freedom to choose from among the published texts. But an ostensible concern for efficiency in a time of economic deprivation and a shortage of paper (and a more covertly expressed concern for the ideological excesses of some texts) led to a more centralized monitoring process.

Accompanying the liberation of teaching materials were extensive structural reforms, including the breakdown of the old tracking system, the introduction of coeducation, the extension of compulsory education through ninth grade, the promotion of new comprehensive high schools, the expansion of higher education, and the relaxation of the regulations controlling private-sector school establishment (but the state still denied support to private schools).

The U.S. mission's *Report* urged decentralization of the control of education, arguing:

> an educational system, controlled by an entrenched bureaucracy recruited from a narrow group, which reduces the chances of promotion on merit, which provides little opportunity for investigation and research, and which refuses to tolerate criticism, deprives itself automatically of the means of progress. (U.S. Education Mission to Japan 1946, p. 4)

The mission encouraged the formation of PTAs, professional associations for teachers, teachers unions, and locally elected school boards. All but the last reform were carried out successfully. After a brief experiment with elections of local school boards, the Diet reversed the procedure and allowed for appointed boards. But the locus for appointments is the prefectural governor rather than the central ministry. Today there are more than 5,000 local boards, which suggests some progress was made toward shifting control downward.

The *Report* was particularly concerned with the intrusion of government authorities into the classroom:

> We have seen that the effects of the old regime are manifest in the teaching practices. Teachers have been told exactly what to teach and how to teach it. Teaching has been, by and large, formal and stereotyped. To prevent any deviation from the prescribed content and form, inspectors have been charged with the duty of seeing that printed instructions were followed to the letter. Such a system has the effect of putting teaching in a strait jacket. . . .
>
> If the teacher is given sufficient freedom, he will make use of many facilities outside the school to enrich the learning of pupils. Farms, factories, offices, libraries, museums and hospitals provide educational opportunities. In some cases where classes are too large, a teacher skilled in democratic processes can call upon student leadership, breaking up the class into smaller groups under student chairmen. (p. 23)

Thus, especially in the early years of the Occupation, teachers were encouraged to join unions and even to enter into collective bargaining with the government for better remuneration (though this latter privilege was later circumvented). Eventually the teachers formed the highly militant and idealistic Japan Teachers Union, which for much of the postwar period has been the main force for preserving the spirit of the Occupation's reforms. In 1952 this union issued a code of ethics that stressed the following principles:

- Teachers shall fight for equal opportunity in education.
- Teachers shall protect peace.
- Teachers shall allow no infringements on freedom in education.
- Teachers shall fight side by side with parents against corruption in society and shall create a new culture.

Many attempts at reform and counter-reform have been made since the time of the occupation, but in most instances these have failed. Contemporary Japanese education is much like U.S. education 40 years ago, albeit better funded and with more qualified teachers and a more thoughtful and efficient administrative system. The solidarity of teachers and their continuing commitment to the postwar democratic reforms provide the key to whatever success Japan has achieved in education for democracy.

A number of case studies and surveys have described what goes on in Japanese schools, and the effect these experiences have on Japanese young people. In my writings, I suggest that the Japanese school experience is remarkably egalitarian. Schools across the nation have similar facilities and are equally supplied with qualified teachers. A comparison of per-student expenditures across school districts reveals remarkably little variation, and this is almost totally explained by cost of living and hardship differentials. But just as important as these external factors are the egalitarian practices in school and classroom management. For example, streaming or tracking is rigorously opposed. All children within a particular school (essentially through senior high) experience a common education.

Within the classrooms, teachers exert impressive efforts to include every child in the classroom routines and seem especially concerned to avoid discrimination against slow learners or children from deprived homes. Teachers form mixed ability groups and work hard to promote cooperative learning and mutual respect among students. Teachers are usually effective in enlisting pupil cooperation in their egalitarian pedagogical routines.

Japanese schools also are democratic, if by that we mean they provide room for meaningful student participation in school affairs. Perhaps most impressive is the level of responsibility Japanese school children have in such matters as calling roll, preparing and serving lunches, cleaning the school buildings, running the school broadcasting system, planning and operating such school functions as sports and culture day, and running an extensive and rewarding array of student clubs.

213

Just as important, Japanese children study in schools where the adults are "democratic" — that is, decisions on most matters are realized with full discussion between the principals and the teachers. Parents also have input. And so the children see democracy in action at the school level.

In sum, the Japanese education experience is egalitarian, and it also accomplishes much in the cognitive and experiential dimensions of democratic education. However, the Japanese school is weak in promoting the individualism that seems to be a strong theme in Western discussions of democratic education.

Elsewhere I have argued that these reforms have had a profound impact on postwar Japanese society (Cummings 1980). The key success of the reforms was in the establishment of more egalitarian educational conditions and in promoting an egalitarian spirit in young people. Social surveys indicate that this new spirit has stayed with these young people as they have moved into adult society and workplaces. Over the postwar period, there have been many egalitarian shifts in the distribution of rewards, such as increased equality in the distribution of income, social prestige, and social mobility. All of these can plausibly be linked to the progressive influence of this new egalitarianism in schools.

But while the new egalitarianism has had a major impact on the social class structure, its impact on gender role differentiation is less profound. In the new education system, both boys and girls sit in the same classrooms and study largely the same materials. In most subjects up through at least junior high school, girls perform on a par with boys. But over the course of adolescent socialization, many young girls, apparently because of the influence of such nonschool experiences as parental advice, begin to modify their occupational ambitions and start thinking more of education and career paths that will prepare them for the roles of motherhood and dutiful spouse. There is much debate concerning the extent to which girls opt out of equality. For example, Sumiko Iwao (1992) implies that most young women today reject the traditional mold in favor of fulfillment in the workplace, thus causing big problems for young men who seek the ideal wife. But her claims may be exaggerated.

214

The conversion from a militaristic to a pacifistic orientation is a second impressive accomplishment of postwar education. Surveys indicate that only a small minority of Japanese young people support the use of force to solve international problems, and similarly a minority express willingness to take up arms to defend their country. While Western philosophers of democratic education seldom mention peace in their discourse, it is a major component in Japanese thinking. For most Japanese, a democratic nation is one that practices dialogue and consensus in the solution of both domestic and international problems. War has no place in a democratic world order.

Concerning other "democratic" effects, the arguments are not as strong. Postwar school education has taught young people to value the democratic process. But postwar politics has been less than enthralling. Thus it would seem that apathy is common among young people and apparently increasing. Through the 1970s, young people, in direct proportion to the number of years they stayed in school, were more likely to vote for the progressive (communist, socialist, and democratic socialist) political parties, which might be viewed as an indication of their critical attitude to the status quo. But in recent years, this tendency of youthful support of the left has largely disappeared. Rather, young people, more appalled by everyday politics than earlier generations, now seem to withdraw from the political process and often abstain from voting (Curtis 1988).

Finally, there is little encouraging news that can be conveyed about the effect of postwar education on the cultivation of individualism and a spirit of independent political inquiry. Young people do seem more independent and critical. But except for a period of heightened awareness in the late 1960s, when the young people focused their critical attention on political issues, they generally have tended to be apathetic.

*Recent Reforms.* The major push for democratic education reached its peak in Japan during the 1970s, and since then interest has subsided roughly parallel to the decline in the influence of the

215

Japan Teachers Union. But the major themes of democratic education now seem to be well entrenched.

In the mid-1980s Prime Minister Nakasone proposed a major investigation of Japanese education with the aim of reducing the influence of exams, enhancing individuality and internationalism, and improving quality. Eventually, major reform reports were issued; and since then there have been some structural and curricular reforms. Few of these bear directly on the theme of democratic education, which merely was firmly reinforced in the reform documents.

However, one important thrust in these reforms was the enhancement of internationalism. Government and private educators have begun to devote considerable resources toward inviting foreign students and teachers to Japanese schools and to supporting Japanese schools overseas. Also — and perhaps disturbing — are the steps that have been taken to develop special schools in Japan to receive those youth who return from study overseas. These children, who usually are the children of corporate executives, are able to come back to special schools that provide them with an easy path toward entrance to leading universities. In other words, by virtue of going overseas, they often are able to avoid the rigorous meritocratic selection to which the typical Japanese youth is subjected. Consequently, internationalism has made a major dent in the Japanese commitment to egalitarianism. Hopefully, the benefits in terms of cultivating a new generation of more internationally aware Japanese outweigh this cost.

There also has been some backsliding with regard to the peace theme. A major theme in the discussion of internationalism is the sensible observation that strong internationalism is best based on a strong feeling of love for one's own country. Read another way, this recommendation opens the door for neonationalism. Indeed, according to the censorship regulation devised by the Ministry of Education, whereas texts were formerly expected to be explicit in detailing Japan's war crimes, they now are required to say less. These changes, albeit modest in nature and certainly modest in terms of their effect on the Japanese pupil's understanding of democracy, have provoked much formal protest from Korea and China. However, these foreign protests may have been motivated primarily by a desire to embarrass Japan, as they grossly exaggerated the magnitude of the changes. The actual texts that reach the hands of young people today are essentially the same as those of 10 years ago. But other nationalistic signs include an increasing number of schools that raise the national flag daily and that sing the national anthem.

Universities never were expected to play a direct role in democratic education. Their major contribution was as a seat of intellectual discourse. Over the past decade, university intellectuals have less frequently resorted to standard doctrinaire political ideologies in articulating their social criticism. Socialist perspectives on national affairs have been displaced by a new realism. At the same time, intellectuals seem to be pioneering in new perspectives on Japan's place in the world. On one hand, some intellectuals articulate the now-prevalent global interest in such issues as human rights, including the rights of children and women. On the other hand, others point out the limitations of these positions, observing that they fail to confront or incorporate the positive features of the Japanese experience.

## An Asian Model?

Japan was the first Asian nation to achieve industrial maturity, but on its heels are several other newly industrialized societies that may equal Japan's accomplishments. In fact, many of these countries share similar development experiences:

- They believe the engine of development is the private sector and that the government's role should be limited primarily to guidance or steering. Their governments have tended to be authoritarian. They have enjoyed exceptional political stability.
- Over time they have slowly expanded political rights, but they prefer a consensual to an adversarial polity. Their record in civil and social rights is less progressive. They prefer private sector and familial approaches in these spheres.

- They have a Confucian cultural base, and they believe it important for these values to be formally conveyed by the schools and by parents. They espouse a holistic educational philosophy, in which cognitive lessons are balanced by moral education and by structured experience. They insist that all children undergo a holistic education in school, and they seek to shape other educational institutions so that they reinforce the school's lessons.
- Democratic education, in their view, should place equal stress on rights and responsibilities. The beginning of democracy is in small groups, such as the classroom and the workplace. As democracy becomes strengthened at the micro-level, it becomes more viable at the macro-level.

These Asian nations, like Japan, are largely excluded from the Western-dominated international club. Often they are the focus of Western criticism, as when Malaysia hangs an Australian drug dealer, or Indonesia uses force to control a riot in Timor, or China suppresses political protest in Tianamen Square. While these nations once suffered in silence, they now increasingly object to the Western criticisms. If the Western formula is right, they ask, then why is the quality of life in the West so suspect?

Singapore, perhaps the most vocal of these nations, can be seen as an example. Since this small island nation gained independence in 1957, Singapore's political leaders have been especially wary of democratization in the absence of economic progress and the emergence of a strong national identity. S. Rajaratnam, one of the senior politicians, has observed: "If Third World societies are not to relapse into anarchy as modernization gathers pace, more and not less authority and discipline are necessary" (Gopinathan 1988). In making this argument, Rajaratnam and other Singaporean leaders frequently point to the success of such Confucian nations as Taiwan, Korea, and Japan during the early decades of their development — as contrasted to various "broken-backed states."

In the early years of the republic, then Prime Minister Lee Kuan Yew argued, "It is basic we understand ourselves; what we are, where we came from, and what life is or should be about and what we want to do. . . . Only when we first know our traditional values can we be quite clear that the Western world is a different system, a different voltage, structured for purposes different from ours." Thus in Singapore the schools are viewed as a vehicle for teaching obedience, discipline, and a sense of national identity. Democratic education, at least as it is understood in the West, is at best a minor theme. The political leaders seek through the schools to develop loyal youth who will dedicate themselves to hard work and commercial gain, not to political action.

Periodically, Singapore holds elections; but the candidates nominated by the government's party are not challenged in many districts. Eventually, it is suggested that more political options will become available. But the immediate task remains a strengthening of national identity and an improvement of economic welfare.

Extrapolating from Singapore's experience, Lee Kuan Yew (1991) has proposed a new perspective on human rights where development is treated as a necessary precondition for democracy. Similarly, Prime Minister Mahatir of Malaysia has raised strong objections to Western-imposed values. This line of reasoning has become a frequent theme in recent regional conferences, as well as in the 1993 Conference of Nonaligned Leaders that took place in Bandung.

Asian leaders seek to articulate a new vision of a good society where primary stress is placed on family and community harmony and security, ensured by a common level of economic rights. Other rights, such as the right to vote, are desirable, insofar as they do not destabilize this vital core. Thus they question the merit of stressing democracy and human rights when such emphasis conflicts with the more basic challenge of improving the material and social dimensions of the quality of life. Japanese political leaders respect this Asian view, as it parallels the first decades of Japan's modernization. But Japan's leaders also highly value the democracy they have built following the tragedy of World War II. Thus in the face of these debates between Asia and the West, Japan's leaders stand in the middle, having experienced both sides.

# Bibliography

Amano Ikuo. *Examinations and Japan's Modernization*. Translated by W.K. Cummings and F.K. Cummings Tokyo: University of Tokyo Press, 1990.

Beer, Lawrence Ward. *Constitutionalism in Asia: Asian Views of the American Influence*. Berkeley: University of California Press, 1979.

Bereday, George, and Matsui, Shigeo. *American Education Through Japanese Eyes*. Honolulu: University Press of Hawaii, 1973.

Berger, Peter L., and Hsin-Huang Michael Hsiao, eds. *In Search of an Asian Development Model*. New Brunswick, N.J.: Transaction, 1988.

Burks, Ardath W. "Japan: The Bellwether of East Asian Human Rights." In *Human Rights in East Asia: A Cultural Perspective*, edited by James C. Hsiung. New York: Paragon House, 1985.

Cummings, William K. "Expansion, Examination Fever, and Equality." In *The Changing Japanese University*, edited by William K. Cummings, Ikuo Amano, and Kazuyuki Kitamura. New York: Praeger, 1979.

Cummings, William. *Education and Equality in Japan*. Princeton, N.J.: Princeton University Press, 1980.

Cummings, William K. "The Egalitarian Transformation of Postwar Japanese Education." *Comparative Education Review* 26 (February 1982): 16-35.

Cummings, William K. "Patterns of Academic Achievement in Japan and the United States." In *Educational Policies in Crisis*, edited by W. Cummings et al. New York: Praeger, 1986.

Cummings, William K. "Samurai Without Swords: Making of the Modern Japanese." In *In the Nation's Image*, edited by Edgar B. Gumbert. Atlanta: Center for Cross-Cultural Education, Georgia State University, 1987.

Cummings, William. "Asian Values Concerning the Individual's Relation to the State as They Relate to the Nature of Social Programs and the Development Process." Mimeographed. Seminar on Asian Values and Development. Honolulu: East-West Center, 1989.

Cummings, William K. "Japan's Science and Engineering Pipeline." In *Windows on Japanese Education*, edited by Edward Beauchamp. New York: Greenwood, 1990.

Cummings, William K. "Examining the Educational Productional Function: U.K., U.S. and Japanese Models." In *International Perspectives in Educational Productivity*, edited by Herbert Walberg and David W. Chapman. Greenwich, Conn.: JAI Press, 1992.

Curtis, Gerald L. *The Japanese Way of Politics*. New York: Columbia University Press, 1988.

Dore, Ronald. *Education in Tokugawa Japan*. Berkeley: University of California Press, 1965.

Duke, Benjamin. "Variations on Democratic Education: Divergent Patterns in Japan and the United States." In *Japanese Schooling: Patterns of Socialization, Equality, and Political Control*, edited by James J. Shields Jr. University Park: Pennsylvania State University Press, 1989.

Goodman, Roger. *Japan's International Youth: The Emergence of a New Class of Schoolchildren*. Oxford: Clarendon Press, 1990.

Gopinathan, S. "Being and Becoming: Education for Values in Singapore." In *The Revival of Values Education in Asia and the West*, edited by William K. Cummings et al. Oxford: Pergamon Press, 1988.

Hall, Ivan. *Mori Arinori*. Cambridge: Harvard University Press, 1978.

Horio Teruhisa. *Educational Thought and Ideology in Modern Japan*. Translated by Stephen Platzer. Tokyo: University of Tokyo Press, 1988.

Hsiung, James, ed. *Human Rights in East Asia: A Cultural Perspective*. New York: Washington Institute Books, Paragon House, 1985.

Iwao Sumiko. *The Japanese Woman*. New York: Free Press, 1992.

James, Estelle, and Benjamin, Gail. *Public Policy and Private Education in Japan*. New York: St. Martin's, 1988.

Kawai Kazuo. *Japan's American Interlude*. Chicago: University of Chicago Press, 1960.

Lee Kuan Yew. "Freedom and Prosperity." *The Economist*, 29 June 1991, pp. 15-18.

Lee, W.O. *Social Change and Educational Problems in Japan, Singapore and Hong Kong*. New York: St. Martin's, 1991.

Ministry of Education, Science, and Culture. *Japan's Modern Educational System: A History of the First Hundred Years*. Translated by W.K. Cummings. Tokyo: Ministry of Education, Science, and Culture, 1980.

Miyanaga, Kumiko. *The Creative Edge: Emerging Individualism in Japan*. New Brunswick, N.J.: Transaction, 1991.

Moore, Barrington. *Social Origins of Dictatorship and Democracy: Lord and Peasant in the Making of the Modern World*. Boston: Beacon Press, 1966.

Nakayama, Shigeru. *Science, Technology and Society in Postwar Japan*. London: Kegan, Paul International, 1991.

Pempel, T.J. *Policy and Politics in Japan*. Philadelphia: Temple University Press, 1982.

Pye, Lucian W. *Asian Power and Politics: The Cultural Dimensions of Authority*. Cambridge, Mass.: Belknap Press, 1985.

Rohlen, Thomas. *Japan's High Schools*. Berkeley: University of California Press, 1983.

Stevenson, Harold W., and Stigler, James W. *The Learning Gap*. New York: Summit Books, 1992.

Tai, Hung-chao, ed. *Confucianism and Economic Development: An Oriental Alternative*. Washington, D.C.: Washington Institute Press, 1989.

Tobin, Joseph J.; Wu, David Y.H.; et al. *Preschool in Three Cultures: Japan, China, and U.S.* New Haven, Conn.: Yale University Press, 1989.

Tomoda, Yasumasa. "Politics and Moral Education in Japan." In *The Revival of Values Education in East and West*, edited by William K. Cummings et al. London: Pergamon, 1988.

U.S. Education Mission to Japan. *Report*. 1946.

Wei-ming, Tu. "A Confucian Perspective on Global Consciousness and Local Awareness." *IHJ Bulletin* 11 (Winter 1991): 1-5.

# ABOUT THE AUTHORS

**William K. Cummings** is professor and director of the Center for Comparative and Global Studies in Education at the University of Buffalo. He is the author of *Education and Equality in Japan* and *The Revival of Values Education in Asia and the West*. His current interests focus on education reform, the Asian education model, and fostering transnational skills.

**Nathan Glazer** is professor of education and sociology emeritus at Harvard University and co-editor of *The Public Interest*. He is the author of *Beyond the Melting Pot*, with Daniel P. Moynihan (1963), *Affirmative Discrimination* (1975), *Ethnic Dilemmas* (1983), and *The Limits of Social Policy* (1989).

**Maxine Greene** is professor of philosophy and education emeritus at Teachers College, Columbia University, where she still teaches. She is a past president of the American Educational Research Association and the Philosophy of Education Society. Her latest books are *The Dialectic of Freedom* and *Releasing Imagination*.

**Abdusalam Gusseinov** is the associate director of the Institute of Philosophy of the Russian Academy of Sciences in Moscow, head of the Department of Ethics at Moscow State University, and deputy editor-in-chief of the magazine, *Rodina* (formerly *USSR*). He is the author of *Great Moralists* (1995), *The Golden Rule* (1988), and *Concise History of Ethics*, with H. Irrlits (1987).

**Kermit L. Hall** is dean of the College of Humanities and professor of history and law at Ohio State University, where he specializes in American constitutional and legal history. He holds a Ph.D. in history from the University of Minnesota and a law degree from Yale University. He is the author of *The Magic Mirror: Law in American History* (1990) and is the editor-in-chief of *The Oxford Companion to the Supreme Court of the United States* (1993).

**Harold Herman** is professor of education and the chair of the Department of Comparative Education at the University of the Western Cape in South Africa, where he formerly served as dean of the Faculty of Education. He is the founding president of the South African Comparative and History of Education Society.

**Joel Kupperman** is a professor of philosophy at the University of Connecticut and has been a visiting fellow at colleges in Oxford and Cambridge and at the Rockefeller Foundation study center at Bellagio. He writes on ethics and social philosophy, and his most recent book is *Character* (1991).

**Wolfgang Mitter** is head of the Department of General and Comparative Education at the German Institute for International Educational Research at Frankfurt am Main and the former director of the institute. He also is a past president of the World Council of Comparative Societies. Mitter has published numerous books and articles on general and comparative education and is managing editor of the journal, *Bildung und Erziehung*.

**Andrew Oldenquist** is professor emeritus of philosophy at Ohio State University. His current research interests are in social and political thought, including the problems of democracy and nationalism. He is the author of *Normative Behavior* (1983) and *The Non-Suicidal Society* (1986).